TWO
become
ONE

*Releasing God's Power for Romance,
Sexual Freedom and Blessings in Marriage*

Harold R. Eberle

WINEPRESS PUBLISHING
YAKIMA, WASHINGTON

TWO BECOME ONE: Releasing God's Power for Romance, Sexual Freedom, and Blessings in Marriage

Copyright © 1993

First Printing   1993
Second Printing 1995

Winepress Publishing Company
P. O. Box 10653
Yakima, WA 98909-1653

Library of Congress Catalog Card Number 92-96962
ISBN 1-882523-04-0

Cataloging in Publication Data

Eberle, Harold R. 1954-
   Two become one: releasing God's power for romance, sexual freedom, and blessings in marriage.
   1. Marriage counseling.   2. Christian marriages.
   I. Title.

                    261.8358

ISBN 1-882523-04-0   92-96962

Cover by Jeff Boettcher
Illustrations by Chris Caprile
Cover Photo by Jean Mahaux, The Image Bank, Inc.

All biblical quotations are taken from the *New American Standard Bible* © 1978, The Lockman Foundation, La Habra, California 90631.

Printed in the United States of America

Dedication and Thanks

My thanks and love first of all belong to my wife who always has been a support to me, even during the lean years. Getting married to you, Linda, was the best thing I ever did in this natural world.

I also would like to thank all those who helped with the typing, editing, and office work needed for the completion of this book, including Ken and Robbie Kolman, Dave and Diane Buchanan, Patty Tipton, Frank Glaspey, and Annette Bradley. Pastor Jim Leuschen added important points to the content and also deserves credit for his wisdom and counsel.

This book is dedicated to my home church which so graciously has been supporting my work and ministry. Bless you all and "Thank you!"

Contents

Introduction   7

1. You Need the Love Buzz   9

2. You and Your Spouse Are a Perfect Fit 17

3. What is Love? Where is the Romance? 25

4. Discover Your Mate by Turning Your Heart 29

5. We Do It and It Works 37

6. Don't Confuse "The Force" with God's Guidance. 47

7. You Can Be Free of Sexual Turmoil 53

8. God Created Sex for Pleasure 63

9. In-Laws, Friends, and Other Obstacles to 69
   Unity in Marriage

10. How to Change Your Spouse 81

11. Imparting Heartfelt Desires into Your Spouse . 95

12. Your Best Opportunity to Improve Yourself . . . 107

13. Attitudes Toward Headship 123

14. The Way Things Work 133

15. Exactly What to Do! 145

Introduction

You can have romance in your life. You can be free of lust and be healthy sexually. If you are married, you and your spouse can be friends and even hot lovers. *It is possible.* I want to show you how.

Chapter 1

You Need
The Love Buzz

A couple in their seventies used to live across the street from my wife and me. They were in love. Regularly, they would bundle up in drab-colored coats, gloves, and hats, then walk around the neighborhood, carefully placing one foot in front of the other. Their wrinkled faces seemed content as they talked to each other and held hands. It blessed our hearts. In retrospect, what stands out to me is how they looked alike. I do not mean identical in facial features, but rather the expressions on their faces fit together. Their countenances emanated the same nature and character. It would be hard to picture them ever being apart.

Some couples just seem to be "one." Of course, they have their individual talents, personality traits, etc., but they are tied together by a deep, invisible bond. This tie is stronger and more encompassing in some marriages than in others. Why? What is this unseen bond and how does it work?

That supernatural bonding is real and it originates with God. Jesus testified to this when He said:

9

Consequently, they are no longer two, but one flesh. What God has joined together, let no man separate.

Matt. 19:6

Notice who does the joining of a couple: God. Two people who come together are not tied together just by an agreement, emotion, written contract, or any other natural commonalty. There is a *supernatural* bond. It is a work of God.

This power which binds two people together is an inescapable force which has universal reaches. After God created the world, He brought Eve to the first man, Adam, and He said:

...and they shall become one flesh.

Gen. 2:24

This was spoken as a divine, creative act. Compare it with God's words, "Let the earth bring forth vegetation," which activated a force to bring forth plant life for the duration of this world. In the same way, God made a declaration for marriage which still has meaning for us today. As surely as there is a law of gravity which causes objects to fall to the earth, there is also an unbreakable law which causes a man and a woman who come together to become a single unit. One statement from the mouth of God created a law for all people, for all time.

GOD

"THE TWO WILL BECOME ONE"

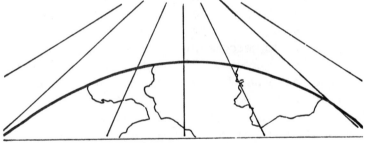

Many Christians have misunderstood this truth. Rather than recognizing an all-encompassing law, they envision a hit-and-miss exercising of God's power. When they read Jesus' words, "What God has joined together, let no man separate. . . ." (Matt. 19:6b), they jump to the conclusion that God joins together some marriages and not others. That is a lie. Of course, God blesses certain marriages, but His binding power works in all relationships. In the beginning God created a law. It is unbreakable. It applies to everyone, regardless of the time period in which they live.

Paul made this clear when he explained how the binding force works even between a man and a harlot who commit adultery.

> Or do you not know that one who joins himself to a harlot is one body with her? For He says, "The two will become one flesh."
>
> I Cor. 6:16

Notice how Paul traces the binding power of God back to the words of God declared in the beginning. The law of becoming one applies to Christians and non-Christians, sexual unions in marriage and outside of marriage. This is not to say that God approves of all unions or marriages. On the contrary, His Word is very clear on the evils of sex outside of marriage. However, it still is true that He created a law which causes people having intercourse to become one.

This law is activated not only during sexual intercourse, but whenever two people turn their hearts toward one another. More will be said about this later, but for now, understand that God's binding force is at work whenever two people desire each other and open up to one another.

What actually happens between two people is that they share their lives. This is not imaginary or just a figure of speech. It is the Christian belief that people consist of more than just a physical body. There is an invisible soul/spirit within each of us. When two people become bonded together, the life of one literally flows into the other. There is an actual interchange—invisible, but real.

We experience God's binding force in many circumstances. When a young couple first are attracted to each other, they actually can feel an energy flowing between them. Many Christians hesitate to use the term "energy" in this fashion, but one can understand this force as we see it linked to God's law released at Creation. Today, when a boy meets a girl and they turn their affections toward each other, there is, indeed, an interchange of life between them. There is an electric excitement in the air. I like to refer to it as the "buzz of love."

THE ENERGY EXCHANGE CAN BE FELT

Unfortunately, married couples often lose this "love buzz," but this does not mean that the supernatural bond has dissolved. A man who divorces his wife, even though they no longer feel any attraction to one another, quickly discovers that the bond still exists. He soon finds out that the woman he has been taking for granted was fulfilling unseen needs within his being, simply by her presence. They may not have felt any emotional attraction for years, but once they separate from one another, they experience intense loneliness. And the loneliness of a divorcee is much greater than the loneliness experienced by a single person who has never bonded in marriage. The supernatural bonding works in every couple's life, and it penetrates deep within a person's conscious and subconscious being.

When married couples separate, they experience the result of breaking God's law. Just ask a divorced person how he or she felt during the dividing period. It does not matter how much they fought or seemed to hate each other. They each still had to go through a "process of tearing." It feels as if a person is having their insides ripped out. Strength is drained away. Life from the other person is extracted. *One becomes two.*

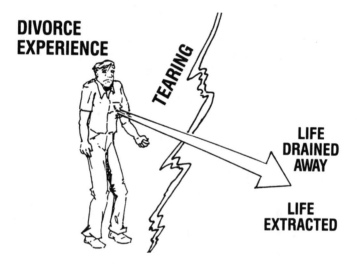

DIVORCE EXPERIENCE

TEARING

LIFE DRAINED AWAY

LIFE EXTRACTED

The longer two people remain together, the more their lives intermingle. One person's thoughts and desires are transmitted to the other person. In time, communication between two can be accomplished with the slightest moving of an eyebrow or twitching of the lips. Each member of a couple can sense, in varying degrees, what the other person is experiencing. The more deeply two people have been bound by God's law, the more they become of one mind and heart. Supernaturally, the life of one person is bound to the life of his or her mate.

LIFE INTERCHANGE

The *Law of Becoming One* is real. People falling in love sense it. Divorcees cannot deny it. Married couples depend upon it. If you are married, then the substance of life from your being is within your mate. And the life of your mate is within you. The Bible shows us how the law of becoming one was released with Adam and Eve, and now extends to all people. Each of us is influenced by it and experiences it in our individual lives.

We will discover in coming pages how you can work with this Law. It will release for your life God's power for romance, sexual freedom, and blessings in marriage. You need to learn how to work with God's Law rather than against it.

Chapter 2

You and Your Spouse Are a Perfect Fit

Twenty years ago, I was a good driver. That was before I met my wife. She has been reading the street signs and highway markers for me for so long, that I am almost oblivious to them. Every few months I will read aloud a sign that I thought was newly constructed, and she will inform me politely that the sign has been there for months or even years.

I'm lost without my sweetheart now. The longer I am with my wife, the more we complement each other. The stronger she is in a certain area, the weaker I become. And vice-versa. It is a supernatural molding that has been taking place.

This is part of becoming one. The more that two married people give themselves to one another, the more complementary they will become. This is exactly what God promised to do when He brought Eve to Adam and said they will become one:

I will make him a helper suitable for him.
Gen. 2:18

The word "suitable" here describes a complementary relationship between a man and a woman whereby they fit together perfectly and complete each other.

If two people truly are one, they do not need to accomplish the same tasks in life, nor have the same abilities. This is easy to understand by comparing it with the way the human body functions. If you reach for your coffee cup with your right hand, you do not need your left hand grabbing it at the same time. The fact that your right and left hand belong to the same body does not mean they act simultaneously, or that one is more or less important than the other. The longer the *Law of Becoming One* has been operating in two people, the more they become one—not in the sense of being identical, but in the way in which their lives intermesh and support each other.

As we proceed, be assured that I do not want to promote co-dependency, a term often used today to describe a helpless, victimized condition into which married people sometimes fall. On the contrary, I hope to develop strong marriage partners, working together in the will of God.

I like to describe this growing relationship as two hands with fingers extended and touching fully together. The longer two people are together, the more they grow in their individual areas of strength. Where one is strong, the other tends to become more and more dependent. Where the first is weak, the second takes on more and more responsibility. As with two hands, with the fingers gradually moving between each other so that the fingers eventually are interlocked, so two people who are one eventually fit together.

All this sounds very idealistic and wonderful. And indeed it is. However, as every couple knows, the perfect complement also can be the perfect enemy. Very often

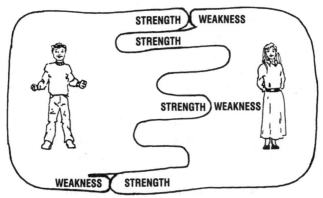

AREAS OF COMPLEMENTARY STRENGTHS AND WEAKNESSES

a couple seems to get "out of sync," or on two different wave lengths, or separated in vision and purpose for some reason. When this happens, the very person who should be complementary becomes diametrically opposed. Everything spoken seems to be interpreted wrongly. Rather than support each other, one person's weaknesses become the exposed targets of attack. Two people who have been molded into one possess the amazing ability either to help (by providing support and offsetting strengths of the other's weaknesses) or hinder (by amplifying and taking advantage of each other's faults). A suitable partner can become a powerful enemy.

Many married couples have not been molded deeply into complementary parts, as we have been describing. We will explain later how this God-given bonding is released with romance and intimacy in marriage. For those couples who do experience this complementary oneness, marriage for them can be either very good or very bad. When they are communicating, everything seems great. When the relationship sometimes slips out of alignment, "everything" seems terrible. This transition can occur quickly. Love and hate are very close to one another. One day things can be great and the next miserable. One day a man may value his bride as the most beautiful creature on the earth, but the next day he can see only her less attractive features. At one moment a wife may be admiring her "knight in shining armor," but the next wondering what she ever saw in the "nerd." The complementary molding process tends to send a marriage toward one extreme or the other.

Not understanding the power of God's molding law has led to many failures in marriage. Let's look at one example of perhaps the most commonly encountered marriage tragedy.

A typical situation is where the husband is pursuing his career. Though there are ups and downs in the couple's marriage, they are molded into two complementary individuals. As the molding forces work, the wife becomes stronger and stronger in the areas of his weakness. She sees the areas in which he needs help and in which he tends toward failure. She becomes, as God promised, a helper suitable for him. He, on the other hand, progresses in his work, becoming more and more efficient and productive. As his energy gets focused toward business, he may become negligent regarding the emotional support which he should be giving to his family, and he may begin overlooking many other concerns in his life. Because those are the very areas evident to his wife, she points them out. Unfortunately, her words are interpreted as antagonistic, rather than as originating from a God-molded helpmate.

Because she points out the very areas that seem un-important to him, rather than praising him in the areas in which he thinks he is excelling, he starts thinking of her as a nag, resisting the very things at which he feels most successful. The scenario spirals downward until she gives up and loses confidence in her husband.

Then one day another woman appears on the scene with a few words of admiration and praise concerning what this man is accomplishing. Suddenly, he feels like he has found someone who will support him—maybe even a woman sent by God. His wife, in contrast, appears to be holding him back from everything he desires to achieve. The tragedy hits when he makes the final decision to leave the one supernaturally designed to complement him and marry the outsider who has not yet been molded to his image. Typically, the result of such divorce and remarriage situations is that the husband does experience a certain amount of success in his career with his new cheerleader at his side. How-ever, soon the molding process begins on her. In addition, the areas which he overlooked (about which his *first* wife warned him) soon catch up and begin to destroy him. Perhaps it is a teenager who rebels and becomes his heartbreak. Or maybe it is his health which he loses, or the collapse of his business due to a relation-ship about which his first wife had warned him. Any of hundreds of problems can emerge . . . all because he did not depend upon his original complement.

One key to a successful marriage is to recognize and accept one's mate as God's perfectly-designed comple-ment. People, not understanding this, reject the wisest counsel they ever could obtain for their lives. Because of insecurities, they react instead of listen. Because of past hurts, couples sometimes take up defensive postures toward one another. As a result, they no longer

can hear the soundest advise available to them. If and
when a person perceives of their mate as antagonistic
rather than complementary, they have succumbed to
a terrible error.

A friend of mine has developed a great working
relationship with his wife. He explained how every now
and then his mind goes blank as to what he should do
next in his daily affairs. He then telephones his wife,
and those are the very times she knows exactly what
he should do next. As soon as she speaks, he immediately realizes how perfect her advice is, so he gets back
on course with his work.

This is how a good marriage should work. Recognize
the supernatural bonding and the complementary
relationships which form. A couple only will enjoy the
full benefits of marriage if they embrace their mate as
their perfectly-designed complement.

Many men are too insecure to depend upon their
wives. It threatens their sense of leadership. Later, we
will discuss the headship role a man is to play in his
marriage, but for now, let me point out that a woman
trusts, admires, and willingly supports a man who listens
to her advice. Developing a relationship of interdepend-
ence strengthens—not weakens—a husband's proper
role in marriage.

One of the greatest blessings came into my marriage
when I admitted that I am blind. I cannot see road signs
very well anymore, but thank God for my wife who sees
them clearly. There are many areas of my own life to
which I am blind. It is because I already have traveled
down a number of dead-end roads in my life that I now
am open to my wife's advice.

This is God's plan for the marriage relationship. There
are two major passages in the Bible that explain how
a man is to be head of his home (I Cor. 11:3-11; Eph.

5:21-33). In both passages we also are told that there must be intersubmission and interdependency.

> However, in the Lord, neither is woman independent of man, nor is man independent of woman.
>
> I Cor. 11:11
>
> ...and be subject to one another in the fear of Christ....
>
> Eph. 5:21

A wise husband depends upon his wife.

I have found that only if a husband listens to his wife does he have a chance at being a success in all the major areas of his life. He may succeed independently in one or two areas, but he never will live a balanced, full life.

There are too many exposed areas in which a man without a complement can be attacked and defeated. There are both natural and spiritual problems which can arise. A husband who does not depend upon his wife is opening himself to being deceived by his own pride and ambition. He gradually can be carried down a road where he misses all the warning signs of coming destruction. Furthermore, the Bible tells us to submit one unto another "in the fear of Christ." Not only is it the danger of self, the devil, or natural concerns that threaten, but Jesus Christ Himself will not allow a man to go on independently of the wife to whom he is joined.

Chapter 3

What is Love?
Where is the Romance?

After God created Adam, He said:

> It is not good for the man to be alone. . . .
>   Gen. 2:18

Over all the rest of His creation, God declared, "It is good." Man by himself, however, was different. He was not complete. He was created with a void in his nature. His condition of being alone was not and is not good.

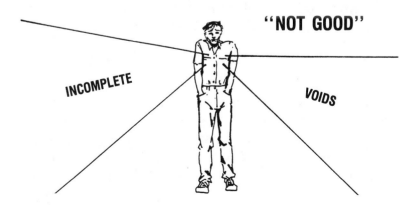

"NOT GOOD"

INCOMPLETE

VOIDS

The reality to man's void must be recognized. Inside of every man (and woman) there is an emptiness that longs to be filled or completed. God's answer to Adam's lack was Eve. The void which existed in man was to be filled by a woman, according to God's plan. Of course, God sovereignly can give a special gift to a person which fills that emptiness and enables him or her to live as a celibate during their life (I Cor. 7:7; Matt. 19:11). However, the vast majority of people always will be incomplete until they become one with a partner in marriage.

Friendships outside of marriage fulfill certain voids within people. In the Bible we read about the relationship of David and Jonathan, concerning whom we are told "...that the soul of Jonathan was knit to the soul of David,..." (I Sam. 18:1). As two people's souls bond one to another, their thoughts and desires become similar. They support each other in many ways. Friendships are important and every person needs relationships outside of marriage.

However, only in a healthy marriage can two people become one. Jesus explained:

> "Have you not read, that He who created them from the beginning made them male and female...and the two shall become one flesh?"
>
> Matt. 19:4b,5

Men and women are creatively designed by God to complete each other. The voids in a man are different than that which is lacking in a woman. A man has what a woman needs and a woman has what a man needs. We have different needs but the longer God's binding law acts upon us, the closer we come to being a whole, complete unit.

When two people talk about falling in love, they are referring to the exchange of life which fills in the voids within them, under God's binding force. As two young people meet and turn their hearts one toward another, life begins to flow between them. That exchange feels good. The buzz is nice. It satisfies the longing within them. When a married couple have a romantic evening and they stare into each other's eyes, the law of God causes a supernatural binding. They are being completed. This is love. It is good.

LOVE

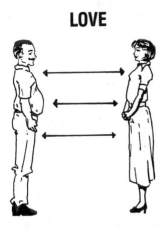

LOVE IS THE EXCHANGE OF LIFE BETWEEN TWO PEOPLE

Notice that our definition of love here is different than the description we read in such passages as I Corinthians 13. The Bible talks about the love of God and the giving of ourselves unselfishly to one another. That form of love is, indeed, God's highest. We, as Christians, must develop unconditional love for our mate and all people. Such love is the fruit of the Holy Spirit, and we should desire to love all people as God does.

However, today when people use the term "love" in

everyday communication, they usually are not referring to God's divine love. Rather, *they are speaking of the energy which flows between two people as they are being bonded together.* When a couple says they are going to "make love," they are speaking of having sexual intercourse. When a woman talks about missing the romance in her marriage, she is saying that there is a void in her being which her husband is not filling. Romance is, in fact, the sensation people feel as life is being exchanged between them. When two people say they are no longer "in love," they are saying that they no longer feel the drawing power between them, as they once did. The word "love" has many meanings to us, but almost all of them extend back to God's creative words, "and two shall become one."

Love is good. Not only is the true unconditional love of God good, but also a blessing is the binding of two people in marriage. This is according to God's plan, design, and law.

What is sad is the state of being alone and incomplete (unless one has the gift to remain single). Loneliness is nothing more than an awareness of the void within one's own being. The single adult who craves to be close to another person is experiencing such feelings because God so created him or her. The couple that has lost the fire in their marriage is missing out on the blessing of God's binding power.

It is God who ordained marital love. It is He who joins us together with our mate. He wants us to enjoy the process fully. You can and should have the buzz in your marriage!

Chapter 4

Discover Your Mate
By Turning Your Heart

How do we become one? How can a married couple, who once were romantically captivated with one another, reactivate those same feelings? Where is the energy that quickens the souls of two people? How can a husband and wife fill the voids that remain within?

God's law of becoming one is released whenever two people turn their hearts toward one another. By "heart," we mean the seat of desires. That which we desire and long for is the object with which we shall become one.

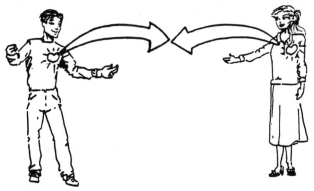

Jesus declared that this principle operates even in a wrong relationship between a man and a woman. He said:

> You have heard that it was said, "You shall not commit adultery"; but I say to you, that everyone who looks upon a woman to lust for her has committed adultery with her already in his heart.
>
>   Matt. 5:27,28

When a man turns his passions toward—and therefore lusts after—a woman who is not his wife, he is committing adultery. In other words, he is becoming one with her. The life and energy from her being is in some measure flowing into him. Whether or not he actually carries out the sexual act, he subjects himself to the laws of becoming one simply by focusing his lusts upon another.

Notice that the binding power of God is loosed not only during sexual intercourse, but whenever one's desires are focused upon another person. Sexual intercourse is, of course, the greatest release of binding power, because it is the climax of passion. Desires become so intense for a brief period, with partners longing for each other, that the binding power is fully activated. To whatever degree a person's heart-desires are directed, to that same degree the binding force works.

At this point some readers may be concerned about illicit relationships or wrong passions that have been a part of their lives in the past. Later we will discuss how an individual can sever and overcome the consequences of such destructive releases of the binding power. Now, however, we want to emphasize how God's binding force can be released properly in the marriage relationship.

As we talk about turning our hearts toward our marriage partner, we do not want to limit our thinking to desire or passion. Our heart is the key that can loose God's power. The heart encompasses everything we treasure and cherish. Therefore, expand your view of the turned heart to include the idea of exposing one's most intimate thoughts, motivations, and desires. Any two people who expose their hearts to one another, whether or not they realize it, are submitting to the binding power of God.

Through the course of daily activities, people turn their hearts and minds toward all their responsibilities and personal concerns. The more demanding a person's job, the more captivated will be his or her attention. As a consequence, when a husband and wife come together at the end of a day, they usually will not be able to redirect their hearts toward each other immediately.

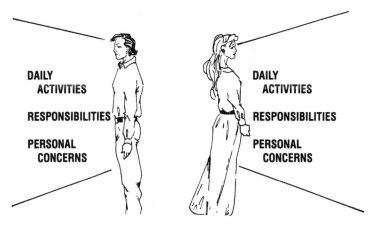

The turning of one's heart and mind toward one's mate is best accomplished in two ways...first by communication. Simply discussing the day's activities and encounters with another person frees them from many of the related concerns. Second, it is beneficial to share some enjoyable activities with one's spouse. If two will go for a walk, read the mail together, listen to music, eat while relaxing, watch a show, or spend time at some other joint activity, their hearts and minds will get on the same wavelength. As they focus on a common goal, their hearts blend together.

COMMON
GOAL

What I want you to recognize here is the *process* involved in two people turning their hearts toward each other. It does not always happen immediately. Simple communication and sharing in a nonstressful activity begins the process. After a couple forgets about their individual lives, they are able to redirect toward one another. They then can communicate on a deeper level. Finally, they will "discover each other," in a much fuller, more personal manner.

Jesus gave us a profound truth when He said:

> ...where your treasure is, there will your heart be also.
>
> Matt. 6:21

Tie this truth together with how the binding force of God is released in the direction of your heart. That person to whom you give your treasure will be the person to whom you will become supernaturally bound.

Do not limit your understanding of "treasure" to material possessions. There are many things that people value more than money. For example, there was one point in my own life when I discovered that my time was my most treasured possession. I guarded over every minute and relegated my time to only the most demanding areas of need. When I learned that my heart goes where my treasure goes, I realized that I had been controlling my own heart and focusing it in the wrong direction. By giving my most valued time to work, I was giving my heart to work. I gave very little time to my wife, and so I found my heart was not with her. The time I did give to her was the leftover moments, during which

I was drained of all my energy and not at my best. The choice part of my day, the most cherished possession I had, was going elsewhere. Now, it is easy for me to see why my love life was diminishing in romance and strength during that period of my life.

What I am telling you is that love will cost you. It is not some insignificant byproduct of life. The fire, the romance, the love buzz, the richness of marital intimacy only can be possessed by the couple willing to sacrifice. What is it that you treasure most in your life? Give it to your mate and you will experience the greatest power in this world—even the passion of love.

Most people cherish above everything else their inner thoughts and desires. They would be more willing to give away their car and food than they would be to expose the deepest motivations within them. Because of fears and insecurities, they will not share their heart-felt desires or communicate them even with their spouse. A person's most cherished possessions typically are not held in the hands, but rather in the heart. By God's grace, we will, as we proceed, help you do this with the one to whom you are married.

Is it any wonder why the twenty-year-old boy and girl who discuss the mysteries of life evening after evening, sharing their deepest thoughts with one another, begin to experience a burning passion so intense that soon nothing can separate them? The more they explore each other's lives, the deeper the binding force reaches. So also in long-standing marital relationships, research has revealed some amazing corresponding facts. It is not Mr. Atlas and Mrs. Model-figure-of-the-year who enjoy the greatest pleasure during sexual intercourse. Rather, it is the two people who have learned to trust each other over the course of many years, and who presently are involved in deep, open communication one with another.

Love is a matter of the heart. It always has been and it always will be.

For the most part, people have a false concept of being totally helpless victims in their experience of love. Though we really do not believe in a "baby-looking" angel shooting arrows of love at his discretion, we have had a cupid mentality. Even Christians too easily slip into a victim attitude, wondering why the love has left their relationship. Not knowing what they can do, they go on day after day accepting the status quo, maybe inwardly wishing for the fire to burn again, but afraid to think about it too long for fear that disillusionment will follow vain longings.

**VICTIM MENTALITY
CONCERNING WHAT
LOVE IS**

I am asking you to change your concept of what love is. It is not some unknowable, uncontrollable force wandering mysteriously in and out of our lives. The love we are talking about is the supernatural exchange of life-energies which happens as a result of God's law. *That law is unchangeable, all-pervading, ever-present. We activate it by turning and exposing our hearts.* We are not puppets waiting for Cupid to shoot us with his arrow. On the contrary, the arrow of God will pierce a person, if he—by an act of his own will—turns his heart toward the one God has given him.

I have found these principles to be true in my own life, and in the lives of many, many others. In order that you might understand and enjoy the fruit in your marriage, in the next chapter I will explain how you actually can kindle romance and yield to God's wonderful power of love. Do not settle for anything less.

Chapter 5

We Do It and It Works

My wife and I "fall out of love" regularly. By this, I do not mean we dislike each other. We always care for one another, but the love wherein the life and excitement is activated sometimes is missing. I get busy with my work and she with hers. Our relationship then seems to drift into a friendship or even a businesslike partnership.

On a regular basis we kindle afresh the fire. The fire does not sustain our marriage. However, our commitment to the marriage calls upon us to keep the fire going. Not only is it necessary, but fire is fun.

We do it like this. Whenever things in our relationship seem "boring," or we feel the symptoms of the voids in our lives, we recognize that it is time to enter deeper into God's binding power. Realize that God's binding law continually functions in every marriage, but if we expose our hearts to our spouses, the intensity and force supernaturally amplifies. Therefore, my sweetheart and I endeavor to share the treasures of our hearts with each other by an act of our wills. We take the time and do it.

Sharing heart treasures is not as easy as it may sound at first. The deep treasures are those thoughts and desires which are buried, guarded, and hidden. When two people first begin talking, they do not communicate immediately on that depth. Usually, husbands and wives only talk about the superficial aspects of life. They report to each other the facts and occurrences of their day, such as what the children did, how their work was, what came in the mail, and to whom they talked during the day. It is only *after* getting beyond those statistics that couples start communicating about their feelings. They may comment about how they felt about the children, work, and people they encountered. After that, couples may or may not go down to the next level, where they keep the root heart-felt motivations of their lives. They seldom open up completely and share their fears, insecurities, and thoughts about God and the meaning of life. Like layers being peeled off of an onion, levels of communication must be penetrated before the

DEEPENING COMMUNICATION

FACTS

FEELINGS

MOTIVATIONS

hearts of two people are exposed fully.

Typically, women are more sensitive in these areas than men. A wife desires to hear her husband's heart. She wants to know what is deep within him. Often the cliche is used, "Men like headlines and women like fineprint." At the end of a normal day of work, a husband may come home and be met at the door by his wife, who is eager to communicate. When she asks, "What did you do today?" all he can think of is, "I worked!" That is not what she wants to hear. In fact, she will not be satisfied until he speaks out of his mouth all the events of his day, with whom he made personal contact, and what captivated his focus since they last communicated. Men, not understanding this, tend to generalize things, while women desire to make true heart contact.

The last thing we want you to conclude is that a person's heart can be probed in a mechanical, step-by-step process. There are many hindrances to the exposing of one's heart. Some couples will be doing great just to share about one of their own feelings now and then. We cannot force people to talk. It is much more complicated than that.

We can, however, create an environment in which we more easily can share our hearts. The plain truth is that two people will not and cannot kindle marital intimacy while they are stressed out or consumed in the daily affairs of life. So long as a man's mind is filled with his work, he will not be able to shift gears and talk. Busy people cannot communicate at deeper levels, and in fact, they rarely even know what they themselves are feeling in their own hearts.

Do not fool yourself. You cannot gaze into your lover's eyes with two or three children demanding your attention. You will not refocus your heart if the telephone is ringing and a thousand things need to be done around the house. No one can relax in the midst of turmoil, and few can relax even in their normal everyday environment.

Kindling love, therefore, requires a breaking from your natural world. Communication demands a letting down and letting go. Soft candlelight, quiet music, dinner out, no children, no phone, and a sense of diminishing responsibiliity all add up to a perfect environment. It is called a "date."

For many, this concept is only a fading, distant memory, now left for the single young people still seeking to win a mate. That is unfortunate. The reality of the situation is that thousands of singles will be giggling and simultaneously burning with passion this coming weekend, because they are doing what married people *should be* doing. They are pursuing each other. If you and your spouse want what you once had years ago, when the fire first started to flare, you will have to do the things you did back then. If you want the fire, put on the kindling.

This advice may seem simplistic, but actually getting married couples to do it is sometimes horrendous. All kinds of excuses flood into the mind of the average person who is extremely busy, or the one who has worn down the cushion on the sofa in front of the television.

The first excuse that husbands give is, "Where can I find the time to go on a date with my wife?" The truth is, of course, that you must *make* the time. It is simply a matter of priorities. Don't shut me off now. Face it. If you want a good marriage, it will (as we already stated) *cost you.* All the time you want is available to you at the other side of your decision.

Most couples also wrestle with a lack of finances, and they cannot conceive of fitting a dinner each week (or some other form of escape) into their budget. In reality, money for a date should not be squeezed out of the funds leftover after the bills and all the other needs. On the contrary, an investment in your marriage must be valued above all those other needs. Your finances should be used according to your priorities.

In our life, we give first to God; then second on our list is the money we need to invest in our marriage. It comes before we make the house payment, or pay the phone bill, or utilities, or taxes, or any other bill. Of course, we are not being ridiculous in this and spending money foolishly on our own pleasures, but in our financial priorities we have elevated our own marriage to the place where it belongs. It is more important than heat, phone, or food.

There have been times, especially when we were younger, when we did not have the money for a fancy night out, or occasionally even to pay a babysitter to watch our children. However, we did whatever we could. My wife sometimes traded her time watching the neighbor's children for their time to watch ours for an evening. Now and then we found ourselves able to scrape together only enough to go for a cheap hamburger. More than once, we have settled for—and enjoyed— an evening stroll. Visiting parks, feeding ducks, walking across bridges, reading a book together, sightseeing. . . have been some of our best times with each other. Lack of money is never an acceptable reason for not spending time together.

The real question relates to priorities and is, "What do you want out of life?" "To buzz or not to buzz?" That is the question! I believe that time and money invested in marital happiness always come back many times over. It may not show up immediately in the checkbook or on the paycheck, but it does come to us. Two people who have a good marriage work better on their jobs. They tend not to waste money on things that can be a substitution for love, such as candy, movie rentals, junk food, cigarettes, alcohol. . . . Contentment in marriage reduces the occurrence of spending sprees, greed, and selfish ambition. Parents in love tend to have less problems with their children, both emotionally and spiritually. Physical and mental health of the entire family is also a byproduct of marital love. When all is said and done, married couples are foolish *not* to invest money and time in their own marriages. It is the most financially sound investment they can make.

My wife and I go on a date regularly. Typically, on a date we do not become infatuated immediately and pour out our souls to one another. On the contrary, it takes time. Usually, I am so involved in my ministry work that I cannot talk about much else for an hour or two. Linda tells me about her work and other natural concerns, as I communicate on that level to her. We both talk about the children a lot and world affairs a little bit. Then after an hour, or two, or three, we finally slow down enough to become more in tune with each other. Sometimes I feel like I am dying inside for a moment or two. All my driven energy is shutting down and shifting its focus from other things toward the person who is my wife.

This transition is not always easy. But as we relax with each other, a blending of our hearts begins. It is only after the intense rush of life escapes out of our grasp that finally we can communicate on deeper levels.

Many times that communication is not accomplished with spoken words, but just through our being together. Sharing an experience together—such as taking a walk or watching a show—seems to help us get on the same wavelength. Forgetting our individual lives brings us into a shared life. Finally, we are able to talk and be together on a deeper level, more aware of each other. We do not always communicate our deepest thoughts, but we try to take enough time at least to reveal our hearts in some measure. Sometimes it takes us a full evening. Occasionally, we do not seem to breakthrough to that place of unity with each other, so we often take a second evening or part of the next day together. We have found that we cannot maintain a truly blessed marriage unless we have such a time about once a week.

An amazing phenomenon takes place every time my wife and I have a blessed evening of communication with each other. In my eyes, she changes. It is supernatural. The woman who just a few hours earlier seemed nice, but perhaps a little humdrum, becomes attractive —even beautiful. It is as if she appears to me to be "without spot or wrinkle." She even starts to glow. Those same feelings I had over twenty years ago, when I first met her, begin rising again within me. There it is! That buzz again. It feels good. She looks good. I feel like a kid again. We laugh and understand each other. I discover that she is a person with needs of her own. By the end of our evening together, I always wonder why we did not do this earlier. It is wonderful.

I do not write all these things to impose my experiences upon other people's lives. I simply share from my own mariage to encourage other married couples. You do not need to duplicate what we do. I have no divine pattern or formula to offer you. It is the binding law of God that I want you to understand.

If I was an investment counselor, I would talk to you about the principles that govern your financial future. If I was an engineer and you wanted to build a bridge, then I would discuss the law of gravity and the other natural forces which must be considered to make the bridge secure. If, on the other hand, I was a fireman, I might explain to you how fire can spread in your home and what must be done to prevent that.

I do not practice any one of those professions. Instead, I am discussing with you marriage and the law that governs it. God established a law. It works in all relationships. I am telling you that if you do with your spouse whatever is necessary to loose the power of love, then you will be blessed.

Let me put it this way: romance in marriage is easy to have. Compare your marital pleasure with an iron used for pressing clothes. It would be very difficult to get the wrinkles out of a shirt if the iron were not plugged into an electrical outlet, and therefore cold. If I want to make the iron function the way it is supposed to work, I have to plug it in and turn it on. In the exact same way, when two people get plugged into each other, things get hot and the wrinkles disappear easily.

The door to marital blessings is your heart. Every couple, any couple, can be passionately in love; not by mechanically taking certain steps, but rather by exposing their hearts, and hence, yielding to the most incredible force upon this earth. A bad marriage can be re-created by the same authority which flowed with God's words when He said, "Let there be light." Even a good marriage can be deepened by releasing this divine power. If you allow the walls around your heart to melt before your mate, you will activate the binding law of God, through which is possible a joy inexpressible.

The manner in which you expose your heart to your spouse depends much upon you. Some people communicate more freely than others. The way a person was raised and individual personality traits play important roles. Often couples have difficulties because of past hurts and present mistakes. We will discuss some of these problems later. Many adults have certain sensitive areas that they simply are unable to share with anyone. As we stated earlier, no one can force another person to reveal the treasures of their heart. Therefore, you have to start from where you are presently.

You and your loved one must get away from the rush of life on a regular basis. Do it this week. Talk about whatever you easily can. If possible, make arrangements to go to a marriage seminar someday, where communication is emphasized. Learn how to talk. Your marriage is worth it. This is the path to marital blessings. The key to love is a four-letter word: talk.

For those couples who are reading these pages together, I would like to ask you to stop a moment and honestly answer the following questions:

1. To what degree are my partner and I experiencing the molding power of God upon our marriage?
2. Is our present level of intimacy and romance satisfying?
3. Have we erected walls in our hearts toward one another?
4. What do we enjoy doing together that draws us closer to one another?

Please take the time to discuss these areas with each other. You may be surprised at what your mate shares with you. It will help your marriage.

Chapter 6

Don't Confuse "The Force" with God's Guidance

You can fall in love with anyone. Of course, there are certain people to whom you are attracted immediately because of physical appearance. There are others to whom you probably would never expose yourself, because your natural judgments of them will not let you. But if you could lower the walls of your heart and expose the treasures within you to another person—any person, you would experience the binding force of God. If you would go farther and focus your desires toward them, you would sense the supernatural exchange of life.

People, for the most part, do not understand this. As we emphasized earlier, they picture God's binding power as a *hit-and-miss operation,* rather than a *law* governing the whole world. Let me explain why the proper understanding of God's all-encompassing law is critical and will help you succeed in life.

Part of my own ministry includes speaking at conferences for church leaders and counseling pastors. One of the problems with which I must deal is the occasional tragedy of pastors falling in love and eventually committing adultery with some woman in their congregation. Typically, it begins with a counseling appointment in which a lonely woman pours out her heart to the caring minister. He, in turn, offers guidance, and while doing so shares some of his inner feelings. After two or three more counseling sessions, the two are telling each other their deepest, most treasured thoughts. Then, just as our Lord explained, their hearts are pointed toward each other, and the law of becoming one is activated.

They sense the force. It feels good. They are attracted, even pulled toward one another. Usually, at that point they experience tremendous guilt and confusion. Their convictions say the relationship is wrong, but they cannot deny the exchange of life going on between them. Not understanding how God's law works, they eventually may conclude, erroneously, that God must be drawing them together. They confuse the drawing force with the will of God.

As a consequence, they may yield to the attraction even farther, finally divorcing their spouses and marrying each other. It is because of this danger that I warn pastors not to share their treasured thoughts with anyone more than they do with their own wives.

Let me say again: you can fall in love with anyone to whom you give the treasures of your heart. Some readers still may question this, because they want to hold to a romantic dream of finding "the perfect one." Of course, God offers guidance to people concerning whom they should marry. There are certain people who complement the voids in our lives more perfectly than others. However, the binding force of God is a law governing all mankind for all time. Any two people who turn their hearts toward one another will experience that force.

This issue is critical in our present society. Years ago, couples lived together and worked with each other for the greatest part of each day. Today, it is common for men and women to work side by side with those to whom they are not married. In stores, restaurants, schools, factories, and professional places of business, employees are put in circumstances where they communicate for hours each day with other than their spouses. This opens the door for thousands of marital failures.

Of course, communication on the job is necessary, and we will not be able to change the whole structure of our society. However, we can *avoid* countless tragedies by *understanding* the law which binds people into one. Christians and non-Christians, alike, must be taught about how the treasured secrets of their heart belong first and foremost to their spouses. Couples can be helped to develop relationships in which their needs are met within their marriage. Also, people must understand that if and when they sense an attraction between themselves and someone with whom they are associating, it does not have to lead to sexual intercourse or marriage. The supernatural attraction *must not* be misconstrued as a directive from God to marry that individual.

This subject will not be complete unless we address the unnatural affections between people of the same sex. Homosexuals and lesbians epitomize the confusion in our world today concerning the misunderstanding about sexual attraction and love.

The Bible tells us:

    For this reason God gave them over to

> degrading passions; for their women ex-
> changed the natural function for that which
> is unnatural, and in the same way also the
> men abandoned the natural function of the
> woman and burned in their desire toward one
> another, men with men committing indecent
> acts and receiving in their own persons the
> due penalty for their error.
>
> Rom. 1:26,27

Make no mistake concerning this. The lusts and passions which are directed toward a person of the same sex are abominable in the sight of God. He destroyed Sodom and Gomorrah for such sins.

Many homosexuals, however, believe that God approves of their sexual relationships. They reason that the attraction they experience for their mate *feels* so good and *seems* so right, that, in fact, it *must be* both good and right. They consciously or unconsciously wrongly think that *God is love* and *this is love, so this must be from God.* They even conclude that God made them homosexuals from birth, otherwise, they would not have the related desires.

In the next chapter, we will discuss how homosexuals, lesbians, and all people who have perverted lusts can bring them under God's order. But for now, simply understand where those sexual attractions between people of the same sex originate. The law of binding into one, we are told, works in adulterous affairs (I Cor. 6:16) and even when a man lusts for a woman (Matt. 5:28). So, also, it is activated when a man turns his passions toward another man. If two people of the same sex look to each other to fill the voids within their beings, they will experience a supernatural force draw-ing them into one.

This is the major point we have been trying to instill. The law of becoming one is, indeed, *a law.* It is just as unbreakable as the law of gravity. If you jump off of a cliff, you are going to hit bottom quickly. Similarly, if two people—any two people—turn their passions toward one another, they will become one. God established this force at Creation.

We must not confuse the operation of *God's law* with *God's will.* Just because two people feel attracted to one another does not mean that God wants them together. This principle operates the same as saying, "Just because a man jumped off of a cliff and hit the ground, does not mean that God wanted him to jump." There is no denying the fact that homosexuals and lesbians find a certain fulfillment in their relationships. They are experiencing the pleasure of becoming one. They are, indeed, yielding to a law created by God, but...."No!" God is not approving of their actions.

To put all this into perspective, we must take one step back. Unnatural desires, adulterous lusts, and all passions outside of marriage are wrong. The place we must exercise self-control is within our own hearts. A man's heart belongs to his wife. A wife's heart belongs to her husband. Even if the passions of one's heart are directed wrongly, the law of binding into one will be activated, no matter what. The *law* cannot be changed—our *hearts* can be.

Marriage in the will of God is the commitment of a man and woman to give their hearts to each other. People should not marry simply because they have feelings of love. They should determine God's choice for their lives, and then *consciously decide* to love the one God gives them. Of course, our chosen mate should be someone we find easy to love. There must be an initial attraction. But we do not *marry* someone because we *love* them. We *love them* and *stay in love* because we are *committed to them in marriage.*

Chapter 7

You Can Be Free of Sexual Turmoil

When we speak of the exchange of life between two people, we are not using merely a figure of speech. God's law of becoming one actually and literally causes the life of one person to flow into the other person. There is an interchange and an exchanging of what I have labeled *life-energies.*

In marriage, the thoughts of one person influence the thoughts of his or her mate. The dreams and visions within one person's heart intermesh with the dreams of the other. A husband and wife cause each other to excel in the very areas that are needed to complement corresponding areas of weakness. Their exchange of life influences their entire being.

This principle is also true in relationships of passion outside of marriage. There is a saying going around today among some sexually promiscuous people: "Every person you are with changes you." In this, even people who do not believe the Bible recognize an undeniable power which causes a person's personality and thoughts to be altered with every sexual encounter.

The Bible warns that sexual sins are the only sins which actually bring outside influences into our bodies.

> Or do you not know that the one who joins himself to a harlot is one body with her? For He says, "The two will become one flesh.". . . Every other sin that a man commits is outside the body, but the immoral man sins against his own body.
>
>   I Cor. 6:16-18

Sexual sins actually bring the life-energies of another person into one's being. No other sin does this. Only sexual passions open the door for one person literally to enter into another person.

In the passage we quoted earlier about homosexual relationships, we also see this supernatural interchange.

> . . .men with men committing indecent acts and receiving in their own persons the due penalty of their error.
>
>   Rom. 1:27

The consequences of sexual passions are not only outward, but they are brought within a person's own being.

This truth is clearly evident in lives today. The case of John is very similar to thousands of others. John watched several pornographic movies as a teenager, and he spent many hours fantasizing about various sexual encounters. At the time, he rationalized that all such "private" activity would be harmless, but now—years later as a Christian—he still has related thoughts embedded within his mind. Visions and images come back to him at the most inappropriate times—even while he is in church or praying privately. Again and again he catches himself focusing upon the sexual features of the women he meets. The time spent passionately lusting, as a teenager, somehow opened the door for evil actually to enter his soul, and hence, influence his behavior today.

Another young man, Tom, was sexually molested several times by his uncle when he was only twelve years old. Now, at age twenty, Tom is confused as to why he feels sexual desires for a man to be close to him. He wonders if he is homosexual by nature, and if he should give in to those drives. He lives in confusion, not understanding where those passions within himself originated.

Sue, on the other hand, is married and has three happy children. For the most part her marriage is good, at least better than average, but she secretly battles with memories of two adulterous relationships she had years ago. The first was only a one-night encounter, but it haunts her and keeps her from fully yielding to her present husband.

Mr. Miller also suffers as a result of previous sexual experiences. From time to time he wakes up with dreams of those past companions. When he makes love with his wife today, he often envisions a woman in his past. His wife has never talked to him about it, but somehow she knows and she feels like she is being cheated.

The list and descriptions could go on and on. God told us in His Word that sexual sins open us to receive within ourselves the sexual sins we commit. He warned us.

Next, we want to deal with the matter of overcoming the consequences of past sexual sins. Until a person goes through a cleansing, they cannot give themselves fully and completely to a new partner in marriage. Millions of people battle the sexual thoughts and visions which they do not want in their minds. Homosexuals, in many cases, received in themselves the nature of another person while they were yet young children. Divorced people often try to get remarried, but find thoughts of their previous mate hindering them. How can these and all the related evils be conquered and expelled from the life of a person wanting to be free?

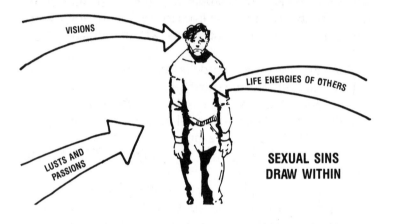

VISIONS

LIFE ENERGIES OF OTHERS

LUSTS AND PASSIONS

SEXUAL SINS DRAW WITHIN

First, let us say that with God there is forgiveness. I John 1:9 tells us:

> If we confess our sins, He is faithful and righteous to forgive us our sins and to cleanse us from all unrighteousness.

There is no sexual sin that God will not forgive. No matter how many times a person has failed, and no matter how disgusting his sexual problems have been, God stands with open arms. For this reason Jesus died on the cross. He took upon Himself the punishment due us and, hence, offers us God's forgiveness.

Now we must deal with another dimension beyond forgiveness. In the verse last quoted, we are told that God not only forgives us, but He also "cleanses us." These are two distinct works. As humans, you and I can forgive each other of some offense, but we can never cleanse each other. God, in contrast, does *both*. He is willing to forget our sins, but He also wants to remove from our being the blemish which sin left behind. He can and will take the scars and darkness caused by even the most wicked sexual sins.

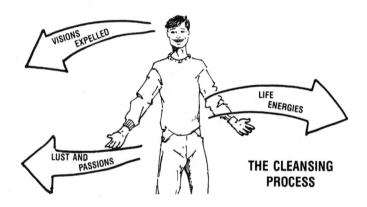

What a person is required to do, as I John 1:9 told us, is to confess his sins to God. This word "confess" does not mean only to speak those things which one has done. "Confess" literally means "to agree with." When we confess, in the biblical sense of the word, we come into full and complete agreement with God concerning what we have done. We admit our sin, but we also take on His way of viewing our sin. We see sin as He sees sin. We let go of our excuses, rationalizations, or any attachment we have had to those sinful acts and thoughts. Then we replace our evil thoughts with His thoughts. *Agreement* means to come into full and whole-hearted exposure of our errors under the bright light of God's nature and holiness. Only as we see Him in this way, are we literally cleansed from those sins which we have committed.

We do not want to minimize the extent of destruction brought forth through sexual sins. Yes, God forgives and cleanses, but *do not be deceived.* Even though some people will be cleansed simply and instantaneously just by speaking out their sins to God, others must go through a great depth of repentance, without which they will not experience a full cleansing.

Mourning often plays an important role in the cleansing of sexual sins. If a person truly sees their sins as God sees them, they will not deal with the issue in a casual manner. Mourning, even intense crying before God, exposes the depth of one's hurts and errors. True mourning activates a process which reaches into the deeper dimensions of one's soul and looses the hold that sin has grasped. The Apostle Paul explained:

> For the sorrow that is according to the will
> of God produces a repentance without regret,
> leading to salvation. . . . For behold what
> earnestness this very thing, this godly sorrow,
> has produced in you. . . .
>
> I Cor. 7:10,11

Many people who have been involved in sexual perversions will not get free until they yield to the deep conviction of the Holy Spirit. This may induce an hour or two of crying, and sometimes even a season of sorrow and repentance lasting several days, weeks, or months.

What we do *not* want to do is *pretend* a person is free, when actually they are not. We want to pursue a literal, actual cleansing, through which God's view of our sin reaches to the very recesses of our being and exposes the darkness. Freedom is nothing less than freedom.

When a person has received into himself or herself the light of God which expels darkness, he or she will hate sin the way God hates sin. As long as an individual still has lingering thoughts of the pleasure of sexual perversions, they are not wholly cleansed. The woman who still treasures deep in her mind the memories of an affair that occurred years earlier, still bears within her the life-energies of her ex-partner. A man who inwardly dreams of someday having an affair is not yet healed. The homosexual who is not disgusted with homosexual thoughts has not yet come into agreement with God, and therefore, is not entirely cleansed. If there is still some desire for a perverse sexual encounter, then that person still has an attachment in the spirit to that evil. Lingering desires and visions are the evidence that the tie has not yet been fully broken.

Cleansing is not always an instantaneous, complete work. Of course, God desires to set every person free, and He often does deliver miraculously. However, most people will be cleansed over a period of time. All should be encouraged to set aside an evening or one other specific time during which they seriously and aggressively—by God's power—rid themselves of the past sins in their lives. The vast majority of wounds and unwanted life-energies of others can be expelled in one period of earnest prayer. Often, however, unwanted thoughts may linger or additional darknesses surface later. Sexual sins are serious. You must deal with them until the cleansing is complete.

The ongoing work can be accomplished by continued confession and taking captive evil thoughts as they arise (II Cor. 10:3-5). Whenever an evil thought or vision returns, the individual simply should confess to God that it is wrong and then cast it out of their mind. *They should not condemn themselves or let guilt take over. They simply must cast down the wrong thoughts and go on with their daily lives, paying special attention to being active and productive during such periods of battle.* Over the course of time, the battle will be won and the scars will be healed entirely. There is total cleansing and freedom available in Jesus Christ, but sometimes a longer period of disciplining one's thoughts is required to achieve total freedom in that area.

The person who has had past sexual partners will not be able to give himself or herself to a spouse fully until all ties to those past companions are broken. Every sexual encounter causes us to become one with the other person involved, and so we supernaturally become tied or connected to them. Those ties can be broken, as we have been describing, through confession, mourning, and despising those past encounters.

It is helpful not only to sever those relationships in your thought life, but also to speak out in the name of Jesus Christ against them. In counseling people through such difficulties, I actually speak out something like, "I sever those ties between (name of the person) and (name of the ex-partner, if known) and all other partners in the name of Jesus." These words are not given as a formula, but only to help those who need to deal with such ties themselves. We, as Christians, have been given by Jesus the power to bind and loose (Matt. 16:19). We can, by faith, loose others, as well as ourselves, from spiritual and natural connections. For the most part, if you need to be set free, you can deal with any past relationship yourself simply and quickly using the name of Jesus. If you need help, find someone to whom you can talk in confidence, and pray with them until you know His liberation.

Such liberation is also important for those who have gone through a divorce. The life-energies of the previous mate remain within the person until the bond in the spirit is broken and the life-energies are extracted. The bond is broken simply by an assertive attitude of one's heart to reject the previous partner.

Finally, it is important that a person distance himself/herself physically from previous partners. Steps should be taken to get a new job, move to a new home, or whatever else is necessary to eliminate contact. If personal communication cannot be avoided, then a guard must be kept on one's heart. Keep the walls up! Do not share any of the treasures of your heart.

Once the tie in the spirit has been broken, the life-energies of those other parties begin to drain away. This is not a pleasurable experience. To have someone's life pulled away leaves within one a longing and a loneliness. It is difficult to put an end to any relationship in which bonding has occurred. It hurts.

However, if a person understands what is going on, he/she can make it through that period. They must allow the cleansing process to occur. *All hope* of ever re-establishing the relationship must be put to *death*. They totally and completely must release those others with whom they have been involved.

It is a deep transition in the heart that we are after. Unless a person has made a decision in their heart, they will not be able to control the thoughts of their mind or the actions of their life. What is required is a decision to reject the energies of others. . . a decision to hate the related sins. . . a decision to keep the walls up. Until a person has completed the cleansing process, they will not be able to act as whole individuals, able to think freely or give themselves in a new relationship fully.

Chapter 8

God Created Sex For Pleasure

We saw the importance and means whereby a person can cleanse his life from past sexual encounters and relationship ties. The reason such sins occur in the first place is because people are trying to fill the voids within themselves. It is not enough, however, to cleanse out those things with which a person wrongly has tried to fill himself or herself. After the "house has been swept clean," there must be a refilling as God intended.

Whether or not an individual has had past sexual problems, God desires to meet present needs through a relationship in biblical marriage, i.e., one man/one woman. A man is not whole until he is one with his wife. Of course, there are exceptions—men and women to whom God has given a gift to remain single (Matt. 19:10-12; I Cor. 7:7). But by far, the vast majority of men and women share Adam's condition. . . if they are alone, it is "not good." God intends for a man to be "filled up" with his wife. And a woman's being needs to be saturated with the life of her husband. Only as two people find fulfillment in each other are the voids eliminated and

wholeness enjoyed. This has implications for our romantic, sexual, companionship, communication, and all
other needs.

A woman's needs are different than a man's in many
areas. For example, she usually desires romantic attention more than a man. This is a God-created void within
her makeup. If her husband does not meet this need,
she may be inhibited sexually and drawn to absorb
herself in other people's relationships, such as those
portrayed in television soap operas, movie personalities,
and gossip of the neighbors' romantic experiences. A
woman with an intimate, rich relationship with her
husband will be less interested in such outside romance.

Too often, partners recognize the differences they see
in their mate, but rather than meet those needs, they
condemn their spouse. For example, men sometimes
ridicule their wives for their interest in soap operas,
rather than fill the related voids. A wife may look at her
husband who has strong sexual drives and think of him
as an "ape," instead of becoming the answer for his
needs. (Did you hear me? I said, "An answer for his
needs.") The voids within a spouse can be considered
either as evil or as opportunities through which two can
become one. A woman has what a man needs. And a
man has what a woman needs. Marital harmony does
not come when we condemn our mate for having certain
needs, but rather when we start meeting those needs.

Another area worth mentioning is the need for security. Women generally have a stronger desire to have a
secure world, where natural provisions always will be
available. Sometimes men condemn their wives for
expressing related concerns. There are even Christian
men who use Bible principles to rebuke their wives,
telling them to trust God and not be so worried. In
reality, God designed women and men to be perfect

complements in this area. *Just as a woman has a void that desires security, men have a void which will be filled only by providing security.* Until both are being fulfilled in marriage, their lives are not entirely good.

The incredible complementary nature between a man and a woman also is evident in the area of beauty. The average woman needs to have a man look at her beauty. It fills a certain void in her to know that a man is captivated by her physical appearance and facial featuares. At the same time, a man is so designed by God that he needs to look upon beauty.

Let me say here that the woman's beauty to which we refer is not limited to her natural features, nor her skillful cosmetic work. Of course, a man desires his wife to look her best, and she will receive pleasure by doing so. But the beauty which a man needs to see—and which a woman needs to have seen—is that which is revealed only to the eyes of love.

I related earlier an illustration from my own marriage . . . how my wife and I regularly share an evening communicating what's on our hearts, and then at the end of our time together, everything seems to change. In my eyes, her countenance seems to glow. To me, she appears to be without spot or wrinkle. It is in that supernatural condition of oneness and unity that, in my sight, she seems more beautiful than any other woman upon this earth.

Only under the release of God's law of becoming one is there an interchange of such life that it satisfies the need for beauty to be seen. I dare say that the only perfectly beautiful woman is the one who is seen in the eyes of a man "under the influence" of love. Of course, there is a natural beauty which offers a certain level of pleasure, but only the man feeding on the radiance of his bride can satisfy the hunger within. This is the completion of both his and her needs.

If a man or woman is not having his/her needs met in these areas, each will be tempted to satisfy them outside of marriage. A man who does not give his wife the romantic attention she needs, will himself have wandering eyes, searching the faces of other women in an effort to fill the longing within to behold beauty. A woman will long for the attention of others, and if possible, try to win their glances by natural efforts. If she is unable to win their admiration, the void left unfilled may drive her to compulsive behaviors or periods of depression. Of course, this is no excuse for a lack of self-control. But here we are emphasizing that sin is resisted more easily by one who is finding fulfillment in marriage. Only the man and woman who are one will be whole.

When two people yield to the power of becoming one, they become whole individuals. As whole people, they no longer have voids longing to be filled. Temptations to satisfy those areas wrongfully lose their power. A whole person is a strong person.

This is vital for a person simply to stay sexually pure. Other than self-control, the best protection a person has from the temptation to satisfy sexual drives wrong-fully is to fill himself with his lifetime companion. Paul gave this advice:

> . . . for it is better to marry than to burn.
>
> I Cor. 7:9

This may sound simplistic, but the truth is that the best cure for burning is a good sex life. This is important!

Let me say it again: the solution to lust problems, according to the Bible, is romance and a good sex life. Sometimes Christians misunderstand this. Trying to be "spiritual," they want to conquer their natural desires. For example, I talked with one couple engaged to be married, but they decided to put off the wedding until they could completely control their sexual urges. That is foolish and wrong. What they need to do is follow Paul's instructions, get married and start having fun. Some people who are dating *should* end their relationship because it is too focused on the physical, but we also must realize that healthy sexual relations within a marriage solves many problems.

To think this way, you must have a biblical concept of sex. The primary purpose of sex is to make two people into one. Sex was not created by God simply for the purpose of bringing forth children. Even if a married couple cannot have children, they will need and should have a good sex life. During the act of intercourse, two people's desires are focused upon each other to such intensity that the life of one flows into the other. This satisfies the voids within men and women, so their condition of being alone, empty, and "not good" is solved. This is the primary purpose of sex.

Whoever said, "The way to a man's heart is through his stomach"? Obviously, they had a boring marriage. That statement is neither biblical nor true. It may be good advice to give to your teenage daughter when she is trying to find a husband. But married people need to be a little smarter than that. Of course, eating together is important, and in a relaxed, pleasurable environment, the bonding powers work, but there is more to marriage than food. At the core of a good marriage is a good sex life. Sex was created for pleasure. God made sex so married people could have fun.

Look at the Bible's description of how a man should enjoy his wife physically:

> Drink water from your own cistern,
> And fresh water from your own well. . . .
> Let your fountain be blessed,

> And rejoice in the wife of your youth.
> As a loving hind and a graceful doe,
> Let her breasts satisfy you at all times;
> Be exhilarated always with her love
>
> Prov. 5:15-19

Meditate on the word "exhilarated." Then read the Song of Solomon in the Bible and notice the romance and passion in a godly marriage. Notice that I said "godly marriage." Godly marriages are passionate marriages. What we see in the Bible are two people feeding upon and filling themselves up with each other—even intoxicated with love. This is God's desire for marriage.

Of course, the perfect sex life does not just happen instantaneously between a husband and wife. There are numerous frustrations and problems that couples may experience. Most marriages go through periods when their sexual relations are inhibited in some way. Let it be known that a good sex life requires time and patience to develop.

In counseling people with problems in this area, I have found the Apostle Paul's advice the best and most common solution:

> The wife does not have authority over her own body, but the husband does; and likewise also the husband does not have authority over his own body, but the wife does. Stop depriving one another. . . .   I Cor. 7:4,5

Of course, patience with an inhibited partner is essential. But basically, a good sex life is achieved when people "die" to their rights over their own bodies and begin giving themselves. Simply do it. Get your motor running and keep it running. What else can I say? It is good advice. Just do it. I said, "Stop complaining and start enjoying."

Chapter 9

In-Laws, Friends, and Other Obstacles to Unity in Marriage

The Creation law of becoming one always is working upon two people during their relationship, but its force intensifies during specific periods. When couples share daily struggles and face trials together, they are being molded supernaturally to one another. Similarly, working together and focusing upon a common goal releases the power. In the same way, whenever two people relax

SHARING STRUGGLES
FACING TRIALS
FOCUSING ON COMMON GOAL
WORKING TOGETHER
RELAXING, EATING
LAUGHING, TALKING
SEXUAL INTIMACY

in each other's presence, eating together, laughing with each other, and letting down their own defenses, the binding power is working. As we have explained, perhaps the greatest releases come during sexual intercourse and when two people expose their hearts to each other through open communication.

Many couples resist the binding force of God. Of course, no one can fight the supernatural power entirely, but often individuals in a relationship hold back a part of themselves. They can sense a force drawing them into oneness with their mate, but they fight it and to some extent succeed in shielding themselves from being pulled too close. Some aspect of their heart, character, or thought life remains distinct and separate.

RESISTING
THE
BINDING
FORCE

There is a countless number of reasons why people do this. There may be deep-seated reservations within a person as to whether or not they really want to become one with the person to whom they are married. Subconsciously, they may be thinking, "I will only bond superficially to my spouse in case I break up later." A past hurt leading to mistrust can cause one to guard his or her heart. Some adults have dreams and goals in life that they feel will be hindered, or even stolen from them, if they totally expose themselves. Others can sense that a certain element in their own character will change if they become one with their mate. Some do not believe their marriage will last anyway, so they hold back.

To become completely one requires a total yielding, a complete letting go of oneself into the care and very being of the other. A sense of losing control, therefore, can cause a person to resist, because it is a fearful thing to lose control of one's own life. Whenever people lock inside their mind or heart some aspect of themselves which they do not want to share, for whatever reason, they limit the binding force.

No one can be coerced to become one with another person. It takes time to overcome mistrusts and deep-rooted fears. There is an ongoing process which deepens and intensifies the bond as the years go by in marriage. One step at a time, the unifying process must continue.

Often the reason two people resist becoming one is because of a third party outside of their marriage. This is one of the leading causes of marital conflict and destruction. For this reason, we must look more closely at this problem and its solution.

Often the third party is a friend of the husband or wife. A man who has formed strong bonds with some buddies, for example on a football team, in the military service, or on the job, may cling to those relationships to a degree that he cannot give himself fully to his wife, even years later. Similarly, a wife who has had a long-standing girlfriend may be unwilling to give herself entirely to her husband, because she holds aside some aspect of herself in order to maintain her outside relationship. Married people sometimes feel as if they would be betraying their relationship with a certain friend if they gave themselves entirely to their spouse. As a consequence, the two who are called to be one in marriage are hindered.

Friendships outside of marriage are neither wrong nor evil. Such relationships are important if a person is to remain mentally and emotionally healthy. They become a destructive element when they interfere with the oneness God intended for the marriage. If one partner feels cheated because his or her mate is holding back, then the third-party relationship should be ended. If a woman is jealous over her husband's friends, then he is most likely guilty of cheating her out of what truly belongs to her. The marriage relationship must be given priority. God said, "The two shall become one." He did not say three or four shall become one. God did not intend for a wife to become one with her husband, plus his six buddies. A man should not have to fight his wife for the loyalty she gives to her girlfriend. The marriage that is in God's will places one's mate above all outside influences.

The third party can be a family member. Such ties can be maintained through ongoing communication and visitation, or they may be simply in thought and heart. The wife who clings to doing what her mother did may be resisting the binding power of God to become one with her husband. The man who holds tenaciously to values which his father held may be resisting the molding process with his wife. God said, "...a man shall leave his father and his mother, and shall cleave to his wife" (Gen. 2:24a). Unless there is a severing of relationships with parents, brothers, and sisters, a person cannot become one with his or her mate.

Often, this requires a separation of physical distance, with the breaking of regular communication, especially in the case of a domineering parent. Other times, it demands a severing of one's affections and thoughts. Of course, relationships with family members are not wrong, and in fact, one always should honor and respect his parents. However, the marriage relationship must be given priority, and when outside relationships interfere with marital oneness, they must be sacrificed.

One's own children can be just as destructive to the unity of marriage. Difficulties arise when one parent allows a child to fill the voids that his or her mate is meant to fill, or when one parent starts siding with a child within the family. Sometimes a wife will feel her husband is being unjust to a certain child, and she will take up the child's cause, to the extent of forming a team against the father. Such problems are compounded and almost inescapable in situations where divorced people remarry, bringing in the children from the previous marriage.

Again, we need to say that God's intentions are for "two" to become one. Children are not part of that oneness. *They are and always must be outsiders to the marriage, while being insiders to the family.* The most loving thing parents can do for their children is to be one with each other. Anytime that oneness is disrupted by a stronger relationship between a parent and child, problems arise, and the ultimate outcome is destructive for both parents and child. If a child is allowed to bond deeper with his or her parent than those parents are bonded to one another, that child eventually will have emotional problems in life. A healthy family has parents who maintain oneness according to God's plan.

In establishing right family relationships, an investment of time is required. Married people must spend time with each other, but also the bond between parent and child must be given attention. A parent who is estranged from a child can restore that relationship. This is especially important in the situation where children from a previous marriage are brought into a new family. Usually, the natural parent has no problem keeping strong bonds with his or her own children. It is the stepparent who needs to establish the parent/child relationship. That relationshp requires time. An antagonistic child can be drawn in by one-with-one attention. Just as communication, exposing one's heart, sharing a common goal, laughing, etc., bond married people, so also parents and children become bonded to one another in the same way. It is difficult to create this bonding in stressful environments or when the natural parent is around all the time. It is best, therefore, for the new parent to spend some relaxed time with the child without the natural parent present. With a little extra care, a healthy relationship can be formed.

In saying this, we are encouraging proper parent/child

relationships. But please keep in mind that the marriage relationship is the priority, and it is there where oneness must be cultivated.

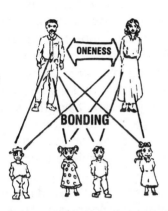

In addition to family relationships, some people need to be instructed concerning the relationships they form with their own animals. I have met several people who have bonded to their cats, dogs, or horses to such a degree that they are hindered in their relationship with their spouse. This is not to say that pets are bad. Of course, animals can fill certain needs in people's hearts. Furthermore, the man who is not meeting his wife's emotional needs should not expect his wife to get rid of her cherished animals. However, if those animals are more important than the marital relationship, then they ought to be removed. They are animals.

As we teach these principles, we do not want to sound legalistic or too extreme on these points. There are times when animals are a gift from God, to help a person be healed emotionally. There are also cases where special attention must be given to certain children, family members, and friends. Yes, there are exceptions. But those are temporary and under special circumstances.

At the same time that we recognize exceptions, we must be firm and clear as to God's order for marriage. Too many people reject God's plan and cling to outside relationships that ultimately bring a curse upon their own marriage. Outside relationships are one of the leading causes reported in divorce today. Unless people live according to God's design, they should not expect to receive His blessings. It is that simple. As a man sows, so shall he reap (Gal. 6:7). If one is sowing a poor, half-committed relationship, he or she will reap a bad marriage. Too many people refuse to face this reality.

There is no great mystery concerning how to have a good marriage. The idea that a good marriage is hard to achieve is a blatant lie. A good marriage is as easy to cultivate today as it has been in any generation. All one has to do is what God instructs us to do.

I once assembled a battery-operated toy for my son, and it did not work properly because I failed to follow the instructions provided. I put pieces where they did not belong. When I disassembled the toy and put it back together, according to the instructions, it worked great.

In the exact same way, marriage *works* when assembled according to the Instruction Manual. God's power is directed toward two people becoming one. When married people resist becoming one, they resist God's power. When they yield and give themselves fully to the molding process, they also submit to the blessings and the hand of God Himself. A man must leave his father and mother; a person must sever relationships which interfere with their marital unity. Two must become one. They must yield and work *with* God's power, rather than *against* it. It is that simple. It really is!

Some would make excuses at this point and say that it cannot be so easy. They hesitate and rationalize as to why they cannot sever certain outside relationships. They do not want to hurt an old buddy. They do not want to offend their sweet mother. And worst of all, they make the ultimate marital mistake sooner or later, by replying, "Yes," when an old chum from years ago (or even their own brother) comes knocking on the door with no place to live. . .followed by a request for a bed for the night, which soon extends into a stay lasting days, then weeks, then months.

To those who would value their outside relationships more than their marriages, understand that you will get in life what you want out of life. When your marriage is on the rocks someday, remember this: "I told you so!" If you do not value your marriage, you never will have a valuable marriage. By the way, there is no *nice* way to break off an interfering relationship. Severing is severing. Sacrificing is sacrificing. This is not a matter of being nice. It is one of priorities and bringing your life into alignment with God's blessings.

I have come to believe that the only relationships which are really positive and constructive to a good marriage are those with others who have good marriages. Any and every couple will have marital difficulties if they are surrounded by friends who are divorced and others who have bad marriages. We become as the people we hang around. Their attitudes and values influence us.

I do not want to sound condemning of those who have marriage difficulties or of those who have gone through a divorce. I am hoping simply to help people face basic realities. If you have a good, strong, blessed marriage, then associate with whomever you like and help them the best you can. But if your marriage needs improving, select your friends with the utmost care. Friends—no matter how great they are—who are not one with their mates, have voids in their lives, and they will pull on you to satisfy those areas of lack. If they are not one with their spouse, they will try to become one with you, and hence disrupt the unity you have with your mate. Did you hear that?

YOUR MARRIAGE   **FRIENDS WITH A BAD MARRIAGE**

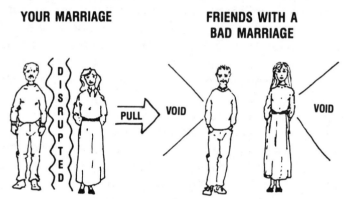

Friends who are not one with their mates have voids in their lives, and they will pull on you to fill those voids.

YOUR MARRIAGE   **FRIENDS WITH A GOOD MARRIAGE**

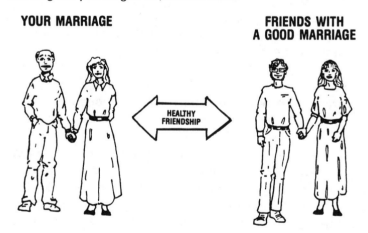

Make your best friends others who have good marriages.

The same principles are true in your relationships with single people. It is good and healthy to draw into your family life single people who are stable and emotionally whole. But if you become one with single adults who have obvious voids in their lives, you are inviting turmoil into your home.

If you try to satisfy their needs, you are not doing them or yourself any favors in the long run. If you want a good marriage, make your best friends stable single people or others with good marriages.

Finally, we want to add here that some Christian groups, perhaps unknowingly, are guilty of violating the sanctity of marriage. We have seen Christians justifying various relationships with others within their religious belief system, to such an extent that those relationships grow more intimate than the marriages involved. Some people have bonded with "prayer partners" or with fellow workers in the ministry. Sometimes a married person becomes very close with a single person in their church. There are also cases in which the leaders of certain churches have been exhorted to commit to each other more fervently than to their mates.

Of course, there may be periods in the Christian walk in which God leads believers to covenant together and work very closely with one another through various projects and problems. However, we have seen many marriages fail because Christians neglected their spouses, claiming that God had established some other relationship within their church organization. Whenever two people begin sharing the treasures of their hearts on a more intimate level than that which is being shared in the marriages of each, then marriage problems are inevitable. Trouble follows down that path. In the long run, we learn that strong churches are made of strong marriages. This must be the priority.

Chapter 10

How to Change
Your Spouse

Husbands and wives train each other. Through constant interaction they teach each other how they expect to be treated and to what they will respond. When my wife and I got married, I thought my domestic chores were finished. I was awakened to reality quickly when, after leaving my dirty clothes in a pile at the end of our bed, they sat there for several days. If I finally had not picked them up myself and thrown them into the laundry basket, I think they still would be there today. When my wife said, "I do," as far as she was concerned, it did not mean, "I pick up your dirty clothes."

Every couple has different areas in which they train each other how to act. However, there are other areas which seem very difficult to change. As every couple knows, these can be points of serious conflict.

Almost every marriage problem in some way involves one partner trying to change his or her spouse. Whether the point of focus is a certain bad habit, character flaw, personality trait, or some physical attribute, the husband or wife comes to a point of intolerance. Couples go at it with varying degrees of intensity, one day demanding instantaneous and radical transformation, the next giving up on the whole issue, concluding that it is useless. A few weeks may pass until some little incident triggers the cycle again. Sometimes at the climax of tension, the threat or escape of divorce enters. For most, the battles carry on year after year, with little or no noticeable improvement.

Picture Tom and Ellen. They are 82 and 79 years old, respectively. After 60 years of marriage, they still live together in their own home, and they still are trying to change each other. Among other things, Tom has been frustrated with the way Ellen leaves the kitchen countertops cluttered with miscellaneous items. Almost every day for 60 years he either has made a sarcastic remark openly or grumbled under his breath as he walks into the kitchen. Before Tom retired, he went to work many mornings with a bad attitude toward his bride, and it was not until several hours into the day that he was able to get his mind on the work at hand. As a result, his health today is worse. His financial situation has suffered. And Ellen is bitter. They rarely talk below the surface. Saddest of all, Tom still thinks he can change Ellen, and someday that she will start cleaning off those countertops.

It is time we take a realistic look at changing our mates. There are two very distinct methods of changing people. Both of these are revealed to us in the Bible. They are seen in how God deals with mankind. The principles of change which God has applied in His relationship with men are the exact same principles which can be used in marriage, or any relationships between people.

In the Old Testament, we see God laying down the law for men to obey. He established certain punishments (consequences) for disobedience and certain blessings (rewards) for doing His will. God removed Himself, to a certain degree, from personal contact with man and demanded that mankind live by the standards He set. He demanded obedience and expected men to change themselves.

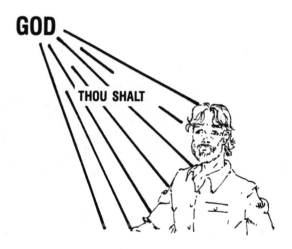

The New Testament focuses upon God's second way of dealing with mankind. He accepted, forgave, loved, and became one by His Spirit with those who expressed faith in Him. He exposed His heart and opened Himself for a personal relationship. God now changes men primarily from the inside, which results in them walking in His ways (outward change).

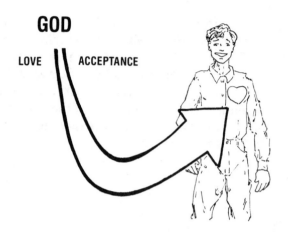

In marriage, partners assume either one or the other of the two roles God has taken. For example, a husband may step back from his relationship with his wife and demand that she live up to certain standards which he deems right (or the roles may be reversed). Either it is stated verbally or implied that if she changes, he will reward her with some natural benefits or with his love and companionship. He sets himself up as judge, and he removes himself from the oneness in marriage.

This type of relationship—with one person demanding the other to live up to certain standards—does not work. It did not work for God in changing men and it does not work in marriage. It leads to rebellion and resentment in the person being forced to change. If pressure is intense enough, outward behavior may be altered temporarily, but inner motivations rarely are.

Furthermore, the marriage being governed by the placing of laws upon one another is *cursed*. The Bible tells us that all who are under the law are under a curse (Gal. 3:10). Too many marriages end with the couple at the conclusion of their lives (if it lasts that long) still complaining to one another about the same problems they faced when they first got married. Remember Tom and Ellen? Their case may seem extreme, but it is mimicked (to various degrees) in marriages again and again. Sad is the picture of the eighty-year-old couple, living together, bitter at each other, still frowning at each other every time some particular behavior is expressed. Fifty or sixty years of marriage have passed, and they continue to pressure each other, never willing to let up. Their whole lives, as a result, have been lived with a curse coming down upon them.

When a couple patterns their relationship after that which is revealed in the New Testament, they discover the blessing of God upon their marriage. If a man will accept his wife as she is and expose his heart to her, endeavoring to fall deeper in love, he will release the binding power of God. Of course, the wife similarly can release this power. Supernaturally, the life-energy of their beings will flow into each other. The desires of one are written upon the heart of the other. Energy is imparted supernaturally to motivate the other to action. Both parties change from the inside first, then outwardly. The longer and more intense their love, the greater will be the release of God's molding power. Furthermore, the marriage in which two people deal with each other in this fashion is under God's grace, rather than a curse.

GRACE

God has chosen the second method in dealing with mankind, and the wise couple will do similarly with one another. There is a power available to us from God, which, when activated, will change the very nature and behavior of the person to whom we are married. When two people try to change each other legalistically, they are demanding that the other use his/her own human strength and willpower to alter his/her behavior. When two people become one, there is an interchange of life between them, and hence, they change supernaturally from the inside by God's molding force.

In showing these two distinct ways of dealing with our mate, we want to encourage all couples to enter willingly into a oneness with each other. However, there is a time in a relationship between two people to assume a legalistic role, where one demands that the other live up to a certain standard. It is with great caution that I include this truth, because couples should be focusing upon and working toward the giving of themselves, as Christ did to the Church. However, even God does not and has not established an open relationship of unity with every human being. Paul explained that there is a time for law:

> Realizing the fact that law is not made for a righteous man, but for those who are lawless and rebellious, for the ungodly and sinners, for the unholy and profane, for those who kill their fathers and mothers, for murderers and immoral men and homosexuals. . . .
>
> I Tim. 1:9,10

The vast majority of marriage problems can be and should be solved by two people yielding themselves to the molding power of love. However, there are some cases with which you must deal by one partner laying down the law and demanding change.

In this book, we are not attempting to say when or in what circumstances a person should give up on the way of oneness and apply a legalistic standard. Realize that in the Bible verse we last quoted, Paul was talking about people who are lawless, murderers, sexual perverts, etc. If a reader questions whether or not his or her relationship has reached such a serious condition, I ask them to seek counsel from a pastor or other Bible-believing, mature Christian.

Having stated that, let's return our attention to where the vast majority of marriages find themselves—two people needing to enter deeper into a relationship of oneness.

In my own marriage, I see these principles in operation all of the time. When my wife does something that annoys me, I can sense myself making a decision as to how to deal with her. My natural tendency sometimes is to get upset and demand that she live up to some expectation of mine. I have learned that this approach never works. In fact, I have seen that whenever I *lock in my mind* something that I think she should do, the fruit is rarely, if ever, good. On the other hand, if I can relax, trust God, and decide that I need to become more one with her, then change is inevitable.

This does not mean that we avoid talking about the subject, because communication is part of becoming one. But the attitude of love and exposing my heart, rather than setting forth a law, produces an outcome with the blessings of God.

It is not enough for us to write about these principles in only a theoretical fashion. We want to explain them clearly enough that you can apply them and determine for yourself how you are presently dealing with your spouse. *It is the heart of a person which determines whether they are dealing with their mate by the Old Testament or New Testament pattern.*

A helpful way to identify the proper heart attitude is

to look at how people change their perspectives as they engage in various affairs of employment. For example, professional people position themselves in an analytical, detached manner to do their work. A medical doctor takes on a detached, objective perspective when he has to do surgery on one of his patients. A salesman comes to work looking for a prospective customer. And a butcher at the slaughterhouse does not feel sorry for the cows he must kill, but rather, he very mechanically and efficiently does what he must.

By contrast, we also could envision each of these professionals relaxing their analytical posture and taking on the involved, open-hearted view. The doctor may sit down and talk with the dying friend with whom he has spent years playing golf. The salesman may see his mother walk into the store and immediately change his heart from making a sale to seeing about her needs. And the butcher could look into those big, soft eyes of the harmless cow and start to regret his own task.

Notice in the above employment situations that we are not saying the detached, analytical view is wrong. There are times when it is important for people to remove themselves and mechanically fulfill their responsibilities.

However, marriage is not such a place. Marriage is not an operating room, salesfloor, or butcher shop. It is wrong for people to treat their spouse in the professional, detached manner. That is much like the Old Testament pattern. To posture oneself in the uncaring, exalted-above-one's-mate position is "to play God" with them. It brings a curse upon the marriage. It hinders the binding force by raising walls within a person's heart. That heart attitude is the very attitude against which we have been warning you.

The heart of the person who is following after the New

Testament pattern does not believe they are exalted above their spouse, but rather on an equal level. As the Word came down from heaven and became flesh, so every person is to "come down from his throne." The proper heart attitude is that which sees one's spouse on the same plane. The heart which releases God's blessings and His power is that which is humble, caring, and nonjudgmental.

EYE TO
EYE

HUMBLE

ON THE SAME
LEVEL

In that attitude a couple must communicate. If a person refuses to talk about what bothers them, anger builds and walls are raised in other areas of their lives. Suppressed anger leads to bitterness or depression. Of course, married people must not be nit-picky or nagging each other, but they only can have a healthy relationship if they talk out their problems.

Many couples refuse to communicate because they are afraid of hurting each other, or they fear that their mate's reaction will cause an upheaval. This is especially true when trying to talk about a sensitive area of conflict.

What needs to be realized is that bad reactions are not caused by communication, but by the attitude of one person to exalt himself or herself over the other. Of course, a wife will react negatively if an angry husband condemns and belittles her. A husband will put up walls if his wife nags in a condescending manner. Bad attitudes produce bad reactions.

What needs to happen is communication that does not cause the listener to get defensive or hurt. Such communication is possible.

First, you must believe in your spouse. If you already have judged your mate as stubborn and unwilling to listen, you have preset the stage for war. Therefore, you must tear down any such judgmental thoughts in your own mind. See your spouse as they really are. He or she may not like what you are going to say, but if you say it right, their heart will respond. It really will!

Second, communicate your feelings. Talk heart to heart. You can try to open the door to their heart with a crowbar or a key. Keys work a whole lot better. So talk from your heart, and let it be known that your words are simply from your perspective. For example, when pointing out that which is making you mad, do not say, "I hate it when you. . . ." Such statements pointed at your spouse are declarations of war. They position you above your mate and your partner automatically is put on the defensive. Instead, talk about yourself. Explain how their actions make you feel. For example, you could start talking by saying, "I feel rejected, or like you do not care about me, when you. . . . It hurts me." Such communication from the heart works like a key.

Finally, relax. Do not talk when you are raging with anger inside. If you are very upset, wait for awhile, lest you say things that cause long-term damage. Do something that changes your focus for a few minutes. Relax.

Listen to some music. Be at peace. Then when you are ready, speak slowly and in a gentle voice. If your spouse starts reacting defensively, slow down. I said, "Slow down!" You are not in a hurry. You have the rest of your lives to communicate. Just talk as one human being to another.

Eye to eye, humble, on the same level—that is the only way to communicate effectively and be one with your spouse. Examine your heart right now. How is it positioned toward your mate? Analytical, detached, exalted above? Or caring, close, and relating personally? The attitude of your heart will mean life or death to your marriage. One attitude releases a curse and the other a blessing upon your relationship. Choose this day what type of relationship you desire.

Finally, let me point out that even the desire to change your spouse should be a *sign* to you that you are not one with your mate. Please consider this carefully. If you are frustrated with your mate, the real problem is not him or her. The real problem is the level of your unity with each other. If you simply will spend some time together, relaxing with each other, laughing and enjoying some activity together, your thoughts and desires will blend with each other. Your evaluation of each other will change—amazing, but true!

You never will solve your problems by trying to change your spouse. If, however, you open yourself up to him or her and start spending some time together, then the areas of frustration will dissolve.

What I am telling you is that every time you start to focus upon some characteristic of your mate which annoys you, the problem is not really their character flaw. The problem is your relationship. It has been too long since you have gone on a date. It has been too long since you have spent an evening together. You are too involved in your business and life in general. Your heart is attached to things other than your spouse.

Frustrations with your spouse are a *symptom* of disunity. Think of those frustrations like an alarm going off in your head, signaling that your relationship is in danger. Focusing on changing your spouse is like listening to an alarm clock, but never waking up and getting out of bed to do something.

Wake up! Don't try to change your spouse. Try to become one with them. The answer to your problem is *not* for your spouse to change. Even if they did change in the ways you wanted, you still would be frustrated. The only answer that solves the problem is time spent becoming one. This is truth. It is important. Open up your heart. Break away from all your daily chores for an evening. Go for a walk together. Get away from the children. Don't talk about your problems. Talk about how pretty the birds are singing or how beautiful the stars are. Sit on the back porch and do nothing for awhile. Watch the grass grow. If possible, look into your spouse's eyes and see what color they are. Fall in love again. Make your marriage a higher priority. You need to go on a romantic date. Enter into the life of your spouse. Listen to them talk from their heart. Nothing else will solve your problem. But love will change everything. This is the only answer that works.

Chapter 11

Imparting Heartfelt Desires into Your Spouse

There is one more principle that we must add to our discussion in the previous chapter on changing our spouse. We have explained how the establishing of laws *does not* work, but the transference of life-energies *does* work. However, sometimes the most deeply held desires of one person are not shared by the other. No matter what a husband or a wife attempts to do, his/her spouse seems uninterested in the things that are most significant to him/her. What can be done in such cases?

Our focus here is upon the overall purpose and philosophy of life to which one person holds deeply, but which is not shared by his or her mate. We are not going to speak about various activities and hobbies, which we expect only one person to enjoy. For example, it is common for men to develop an interest in sports, hunting, fishing, automobiles, etc. Wives are more likely to enjoy shopping, visiting, etc. These differences are normal and we do not expect to change them. It is the deeper-life concerns, i.e. religious beliefs and the way one looks at life, that we hope are shared by both husband and wife. What can be done when one spouse is more zealous for God, a specific church, or the things of God than the other spouse? Too many husbands are sitting at home while their wives are spending their evenings at church activities. Not quite as common, but just as discouraging, is the scene of a man filled with a passion for ministry but his wife is seemingly uninterested. How can the zeal of one be stimulated in the other? How can the most basic issues of life be resolved and shared?

Jesus faced the same dilemma in His relationship with the Church, the Bride to whom He is betrothed. All of us like sheep have gone astray. Jesus, however, is perfection. What was His plan to win us to Himself? How did the desires upon His heart get planted within our hearts? He explained in John 12:24.

> Truly, truly, I say to you, unless a grain of
> wheat falls into the earth and dies, it remains
> by itself alone; but if it dies, it bears much
> fruit.
>
> John 12:24

Jesus made this statement shortly before His death in order to explain what He was about to do. To understand it, examine carefully. The seed was not only His life, but the very purpose for which He was sent into the world. He explained that unless He died, He would remain by Himself alone. However, if He died, that which He was sent to do would bear fruit. It would be planted and fulfilled in the lives of many others.

Jesus used the analogy of a seed dying to explain what would happen in His life, but He implied that it was a principle for our lives, too. Any person who has a spiritual drive within from the Holy Spirit, has the life or a seed from God. However, as Jesus said, that seed, zeal, energy, and vision will remain alone. In other words, the passion and purpose within one person will be limited and not embraced by others.

The only way the seed can be transferred from one heart to another is through death. This does not mean physical death. But the vision within must fall from its position in the heart. Basically, a person must come to the place in his or her life where that passion and zeal is not so important and, in fact, is "dead." The individual must honestly, and to the depth of his or her being, completely release the seed. If this is accomplished, then the seed is planted supernaturally in others—specifically within those to whom one is bonded. The very passion and desires which once were held in one heart are planted in the hearts of others.

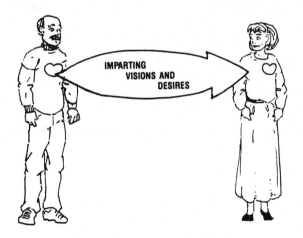

If you are comprehending this, it may sound too good to be true, but it is a real truth which Jesus taught us. Many examples can be found in the Bible to show us how it works. For example, think of Joseph who, as a boy, had a vision from God that he would rule over many nations (Gen. 37). It was not until Joseph had gone through years of imprisonment that his vision was fulfilled. In similar fashion, Moses had a passion to see the Jewish people freed from their captivity. He was so compelled that he killed a certain slave master with his own hands. Moses' desire, however, was not shared by the Jews themselves. Years later, after Moses had spent much of his life in the wilderness, the Jewish slaves began crying out for deliverance. By that time Moses had gone through a complete death to his original passion. When God wanted him to go lead the people, he did not want any part of the task. Such is the process of dying that causes those very desires to bear fruit in the lives of those who should be sharing them.

It was not by application to marriage that I first became convinced of the seed-dying truth, but through my relationship with my elders in the church I pastored. At one point I became consumed with a vision for church growth. I desperately wanted to step out and purchase a new, large church building; but my elders who worked with me could not see the need. They had no interest in doing what I was convinced God was directing us to do. Week after week I talked to them and tried to get them to understand. At times they seemed to have temporary thoughts of support and excitement, but that would pass, and they turned back into "deadweights" that I tried to drag along behind me. Talking could not change them. Logical arguments seemed futile. Prayer somehow must have helped, but I have to admit I saw little or no change within their hearts. At times I got upset with them, other times I was just confused, but all the time I was totally convinced that God wanted us to step out in faith as a church.

Of course, I could have gone on without my elders, declaring that they were resisting the will of God. But before I brushed the dirt from off of my feet, God began to deal with me about my attitude. He drew my attention to the words of Jesus in John 12, about the seed remaining by itself alone until it dies. I was standing alone at that time. I knew God was telling me that I had to die. He was directing me to let the vision go. I had to push it out of my heart and forget it.

This was no small matter for me. I was convinced God wanted us to aggressively advance as a church. At first I battled with my thoughts, wondering if I was abandoning what God had called me to do. I felt guilty. As I began backing down, a few congregational members outside of the eldership questioned me as to whether I was shrinking back from the will of God. I was not sure that what I was doing was totally right. Besides, it was hard! My whole life was wrapped up in that church, and I desired the best for them. Everything in me seemed to resist my resolve to push the vision out of my heart and mind. It was a real death for me.

Finally, I honestly and totally came to the point where I did not care if we ever purchased a new building. That very week I went to my regularly scheduled elders' meeting, and lo and behold, they could not wait to talk about buying a new facility and advancing the church in many other ways. I had a hard time believing it at first. In fact, I did not. But as I realized that the vision had been planted supernaturally in their hearts, I had to resurrect it within me.

Now, before we go on to apply this principle to marriage, I want you to notice the transition that had happened in my own heart. In dying, my vision had been dethroned, but look at what filled that position in my heart. I had decided that my elders were more important

than my vision. I dethroned my vision and put people—
those elders—in that place closest to my heart. When
I was consumed with the vision, without realizing it, I
had, in a sense, ejected my elders from my heart. For
a time, I wanted the vision more than I wanted them.
When I got them back next to my heart, valuing them
above the vision, then that vision took root in their
hearts. Dying successfully, therefore, involves not only
dethroning a vision, but also putting back in that
position those people who should share the vision with
you. *People are more important than purpose.*

Our Lord did this very thing. He was sent to establish
a kingdom. He did not have to die. He could have come
to the earth and ruled with His power over every human
being. But instead He died. Why? To purchase for
Himself a Bride to rule with Him. He put the Bride ahead
of that kingdom vision so that we will fulfill the vision
with Him.

In my own marriage, I see this principle in operation
all the time. Personally, I am a man burning with a
passion to change the world. I love to speak at conferences and churches. I love to write things that impact
lives. It is my call from God. Sometimes, however, I
"lose" my wife. She loves God and supports me, but
occasionally I get moving so fast that I forget her. Not
realizing it, I dethrone her. The ministry God has given
to me creeps up to consume my thoughts and desires.
At that point my wife loses interest in what I am doing.
She tries to keep up, but spiritually I have pushed her
out of her rightful position closest to my heart. When
I was younger, there were times that I became consumed by what I thought God wanted me to do; today
I can look back and see how wrong I was.

You may or may not be able to relate to such a
passion for ministry, but there are other things, such

as work, sports, hobbies, friends, etc., that can captivate your heart totally. That which is exalted in the heart becomes an idol. What I want you to see is that living with a driving passion—even if that passion is focused on God or ministry—can be wrong. Of course, God must be first in every Christian's heart. But in terms of human relationships, people—not purpose—must capture the heart.

Look with a new perspective at the individual who is consumed with a vision and exalts that vision above his or her spouse. God created a man and woman to become one with each other. If the deepest heart passions are directed toward something other than one's spouse, then oneness in marriage is violated. In a sense, adultery is committed. That is a very selfish way to live. Furthermore, it is unfair to one's mate. A person who is clinging to a certain vision (even if that vision is God-inspired) may love it so much that he guards it and keeps it from his or her mate. Walls become erected in their hearts and the deepest treasures never are shared. Unity is impossible. Two people cannot become one when the person of vision is forbidding the other access to his or her heart.

**GUARDING ONE'S
HEART TO PROTECT
CERTAIN DESIRES
AND GOALS**

Again, we need to remind you, only when a person *dies* to their deepest desires can those desires be planted in the hearts of those to whom they are bonded. When the walls are let down and one person exposes his or her heart to the other, a flow of the life-energies begins between the two. Only if the seed dies can it bear fruit.

It is worth mentioning here that these spiritual principles function also in the relationship parents have with their children. Many parents have put their passion to serve God above their own children, and, consequently, those children never share in their parents' spiritual zeal. A similar error is made when a parent formulates plans for their child's future, but later, when that child grows up, he or she begins developing his or her own desires and goals. The parents sometime become more and more determined to force their way upon their growing offspring. The youth then veer farther and farther away. A wedge is driven between the generations, and communication soon seems fruitless. In such cases, what the parents rarely realize is that they have put their *plans* and *desires* for their child *above their child.* Of course, they want the best for their loved one, but even "wanting the best" can be put above the person himself. Typically, though, the parent in such a dilemma eventually gives up and sooner or later decides to love his/her child, regardless of what he or she becomes. It is then that the desires upon the parents' hearts begin to have a positive influence on the character and direction of their children.

Unfortunately, successfully dying is not a one-time experience. The visions and passions upon a person's heart repeatedly must be subjected to a position below love for another. Any individual who is a visionary, goal-oriented type too easily can be drawn back into the state of being driven. The desires to accomplish something must be put to death again and again. Each time a death is completed in one person, conception is brought forth in another. The deeper the death in one partner, the more firmly the seeds become planted in the one to whom they are bonded.

Through trials and mistakes, I have learned that my wife—not my vision—deserves the position closest in my heart. If I notice that my sweetheart is losing interest in my work, I take it as a sign that the idol of ministry has arisen in me again. It is a simple matter to win her back. I repent. I have to dethrone my own goals and plans. I honestly and completely have to set aside my "mission" and refocus my life back upon her. I rediscover who she is and forget my own desires.

This is easier said than done. As I described in an earlier chapter, Linda and I will go on a date. At first, I do not realize how consumed I actually have become in the affairs of ministry. I only see the symptoms of her lonely heart. When we begin to talk, my mind usually is filled with what I want to accomplish next in life. It is great talking to one another about all of that, but it typically takes two or three hours together before I actually can set it all aside and redirect my heart toward her needs and desires. Thoughts shift in my mind as a dethroning, and then an enthroning happens within me.

I have found that the best way to successfully change my heart is to do the things that are on my wife's heart, rather than what I like to do. For example, I am not one who enjoys shopping for clothes or sitting around relaxing. My wife loves to do both. When I do those things with her, I go through a real death. But that is okay. In fact, I have realized that it is good. By doing with her what she likes to do, I am refocusing my life. I am not referring to being a martyr or "suffering" through a time with her. No. I mean making a decision to sacrifice my own desires and deciding to enjoy with her some of her favorite activities. For example, nothing makes me die to my own goals more quickly than walking around a store and looking at clothes. At the same time, nothing else better proves to my wife that I care more about her than I care about my work.

It is when I allow my wife to be the queen within my heart, that she supernaturally becomes interested in helping me to fulfill all that God has called me to do. When she has that place in my heart, then what is on *my* heart is transferred into *her* heart.

In one counseling situation, I spoke with a wife who could not get her husband to share in her passion to do the will of God. All she wanted to do in life was pray and talk to people about the Lord. Her husband, on the other hand, worked hard, was not too interested in ministry, and liked to fish on his days off. The wife went from rebuking her husband. . .to praying for him. . .to giving up on him. What she really needed to do was to make him "king" in her heart (I Pet.3:6), and then go fishing with him. Of course, her story was that she hated to fish, and, besides, it was a waste of God's time. What she did not realize at the time was that fishing was the perfect way to transform her own heart and win her husband. The very act of willfully sacrificing her own goals would have dethroned the idol she had made of ministry. Doing what her husband desired would be valuing him above her own desires and putting him back in his rightful place. Only then can the desires upon her heart actually be transmitted to him. And as Jesus said, the seeds of life within her would be planted in him, eventually to bear fruit.

There is a great truth to the saying, "Your dreams will be fulfilled when you live to fulfill another's dreams."

Recall Joseph and the dream he had to rule over nations (Gen. 37); his dream was not fulfilled until he had spent years as a slave faithfully serving Potiphar, and then as a prisoner where he interpreted the butler's dream and deciphered Pharaoh's dream. So also, this principle is true in marriages today. When a husband and wife set aside their own goals and begin to help their spouse accomplish their visions, then, and only then, will they become one. It is in that servant role that the dreams within one's heart are exalted in the other's. It is supernatural. It is the way God made us.

In conclusion: die. Let go of that which holds your heart apart from your spouse. I said, "Let it go."

Chapter 12

Your Best Opportunity To Improve Yourself

Marriage is the perfect opportunity to improve yourself. There is no other single setting of life that can form more character, patience, and love in the heart of a person than marriage. What is learned in the average marriage will give more to a person than a college education, years working at any career, and all the training that could be obtained in any classroom. In this chapter, we want to convince you that your best opportunity to grow and mature is through your marriage. We are talking about changing yourself for the better.

What we are about to teach stems from our understanding of how God's molding power forms married people into complementary partners. I like to picture the complementary relationship between a man and a woman like a teeter-totter. When one side of the seesaw goes up, the other side lowers. So it is also in a relationship where two people are one. Qualities, strengths, and certain characteristics in life increase in one person, as they simultaneously decrease in the other. Of course,

we are not referring to qualities such as holiness increasing in one person as they decrease in the other.
No. It is primarily those characteristics and strengths
related to responsibility which function in this complementary, seesaw fashion.

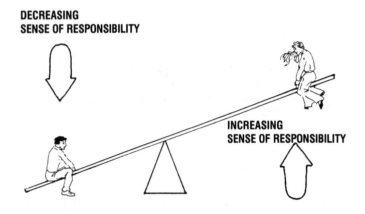

DECREASING
SENSE OF RESPONSIBILITY

INCREASING
SENSE OF RESPONSIBILITY

This principle is so critical and eye-opening that I
want to give you an illustration before we apply it to the
practical aspects of marriage. A few years ago, I was
sightseeing far back in the mountains of Montana, when
I came across a large herd of elk. An intriguing phenomenon became evident as I silently watched them
grazing in the open meadow. In the herd of over one
hundred, there were always about a dozen elk with their
heads raised, carefully watching the surrounding tree-
line for danger. They stood as sentries, alert and sensitive to the slightest movement, while all the rest of the
elk casually walked through the high grasses and
nibbled on the choicest available food. Every few
minutes an amazing transition would take place. Those
elk which were on the lookout for intruders, abruptly

lowered their heads and joined the rest of those calmly grazing. Precisely at that moment of transition, other elk would stop eating and take over the responsibility of guarding from danger. There was no signal nor noise that notified when one elk should relax and another take over. Often the elk were not even within sight of each other. It was fascinating how they functioned as a unit. When one yielded responsibility, another accepted it.

A man and woman who have been married for any length of time have a similar bond between them, in that one complements the other and responsibility is shared. Of course, there are certain obstacles in life that require the attention and energies of both of them. But for the ongoing struggles and details of life, whenever one person takes on more responsibility than he or she should, it diminishes the sense of responsibility in the other. And the opposite also is true. If one person becomes irresponsible in a certain area, it automatically causes a sense of responsibility in that very area to arise in the spirit, mind, and emotions of his or her mate. These forces are good, and they are meant to make life easier, allowing people to work effectively together.

Now, let's see how we can apply this principle properly. George and Tammy have a problem in their home. Tammy does most of the housework and she does a fairly good job, except for keeping the floors clean. She simply cannot get herself to vacuum the carpets or sweep. In fact, she is somewhat oblivious to the need. George, on the other hand, says that clean floors are the number one priority. Therefore, he has tried everything he knows to get Tammy to do the job. In spite of all his efforts, the floors rarely meet his approval.

What can George do? Vacuum the carpets himself. That's right. So long as George is holding the sense of responsibility within him (evident by the fact that dirty floors bother him), he is the one who ought to be doing the work. Tammy will not receive the motivation to do the job until George gets rid of the burden. That is simply how the marriage relationship functions— complementary.

In one marriage I know, this was the very problem they faced. The husband finally stopped trying to change his wife and he started vacuuming. Do you know what he discovered? That he actually enjoyed it, and then he wondered why he had not been doing it all along.

Many marriage problems would dissolve if individuals would simply *act* upon the sense of responsibility that they have, rather than trying to force it upon their spouse. In the preceeding example, the husband tried to coerce his wife to do the vacuuming, because he had been influenced by his traditional understanding of men's and women's roles. It is the molding power of God which causes two people to share the various responsibilities of life. Therefore, roles should be established by one's sense of responsibility, rather than by any traditional mentality. The person who has the burden, normally has the energy to do the related work. If we work contrary to the sense of responsibility, we push against the very power that disbursed that responsibility to us. The plain fact of the matter is that differences between a husband and wife are necessary. That is how two people can be more productive as a team than they can be individually.

There are times that one person is taking on too much responsibility, and that leaves his or her mate irresponsible in a negative way. Picture Bill and Sue's relationship. Bill has been trying zealously to live according to the Bible, but lately he and his wife have been fighting a lot. Sue thinks her husband is being financially irresponsible. Bill can meet the monthly expenses with his present income, but they never have been able to get ahead, and two loans from relatives have been standing unpaid for several years. Bill thinks Sue is just nagging and worrying too much. Over the past few weeks, he has been quoting certain scriptures, implying that she needs to trust God more. Sue goes back and forth, one day feeling condemned, the next outraged at her once beloved companion.

The answer to this dilemma is simple.

Look first at what Bill has been doing. He has been judging his wife for being so worried, while at the same time making himself more and more irresponsible. By the very laws of God which make his wife his complement, she becomes increasingly burdened. Bill thinks it is his wife's problem, when in reality he is the one making her carry the load. The more he fixes in his mind irresponsible thoughts—even if those thoughts are backed by certain Bible verses—the more he releases upon his wife the related sense of responsibility. Bill is misunderstanding what the Bible teaches.

If Bill wants to solve this problem, he must accept the sense of responsibility which his wife carries. That's right. A man is supposed to love his wife as Christ loved the Church. Just as Jesus took on the burdens of His Bride, so also a husband is to accept within himself the weights which are too heavy for his wife. Bill may have a hard time with this concept, because he sees the attitude of his wife as sinful. According to his present way of thinking, it would be wrong for him to "start worrying about money." But the idea we want to communicate is that he must do as Christ does for the Church. Rather than condemn Sue, he needs to listen— actually listen—to her. *Let his wife express her concerns without directing judgment toward her.* Then Bill needs to spend some time thinking about how to solve those problems. Faith is not irresponsibility. Rather, it is facing problems and believing that God will help solve them. Bill needs to set his wife free by taking upon himself the burden. He needs to *make* himself concerned. He will not have to carry the burden in an ungodly fashion. He can, in fact, take it to God. But first he must release his wife from the pressure by letting her communicate her worries, and then consciously increasing his own sense of responsibility in that area.

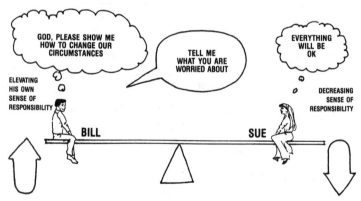

In saying this, we are not justifying Sue's lack of trust in God, nor any unloving attitudes she has had toward Bill. There are things she can do, as well, to remedy the situation. The seesaw works both ways. If she, by an act of her own will, rejects that sense of responsibility weighing upon her, it will begin shifting supernaturally onto her husband. So long as she continues carrying the burden, all her nagging and condemning is in vain. The battle must be fought in her own mind and emotions. If, and only if, she casts down all those thoughts of worry and lack, will he be able to start sensing the burden. This is not just a battle for a moment or two, but Sue may be required to keep it up for weeks or even months—at least until she truly has conquered the thoughts within herself.

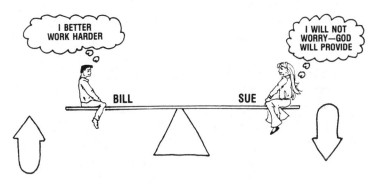

Another area in which these complementary forces are evident pertains to pride and humility. God has ordained a law in this regard.

> And whoever exalts himself shall be humbled;
> and whoever humbles himself shall be exalted.
> Matt. 23:12

This principle applies to every human being, but it often becomes activated within the marriage relationship.

For example, when a man begins to exalt himself, brag about his own accomplishments, exaggerate his achievements, and portray a false image of who he is, there are supernatural forces—from God—which are released to humble him. These humbling forces can work through natural circumstances or other people, but very often they manifest through his marriage partner. Many a proud man has been at the climax of his best story, impressing all his friends, when his wife emerges from the background to spurt out the one perfect statement that puts him back in his place. Typically, the humiliated husband becomes enraged at his beloved, and perhaps later demands to know why she "never supports him!"

In reality, it was the very law of God at work in her, triggered by his arrogance. Of course, we are not justify-ing a wife belittling her husband. That is a serious sin that must not be excused. However, we also must note that the wise man learns quickly that exalting himself in the presence of his wife is dangerous. On the other hand, a man can create a wife who supports and admires him by keeping a realistic view of himself.

Your spouse is an expert on your behavior. There is no human being more qualified to counsel and help you. As we have explained, the molding power of God has been at work on your spouse, forming him or her into the perfect complement for you. Unfortunately, married people usually do not listen to their spouse too willingly or readily. When it comes to revealing char-acter flaws, the last person we want to hear it from is our spouse. If someone else tells us the very same thing, we will be much more receptive. It is difficult to hear it from the one who sleeps in the same bed with you.

However, I want to help you hear. If your mate truly is designed by God to be your complement, then he or she has something to say to you. In fact, I believe that the best mirror into which you can look is the reaction of your mate. I want to help you "read" what is written about yourself on the life of your spouse. It will help you.

The most important thing to know is that when looking into this "human mirror," everything is complementary. Have you ever tried to read something by looking at its reflection in a mirror? It is reversed. Try reading a sign in the rearview mirror of your car some day. That is exactly how marriage reflections work.

For example, we talked about responsibility. If you notice your spouse being irresponsible, that should tell you that you are carrying too much in the related areas. If your spouse is worried and too preoccupied with things, you should check yourself seriously to see if you are being irresponsible.

You also can learn about your own heart by noticing that against which your spouse turns his/her heart. The Bible tells us that the heart is deceptive, and we, ourselves, are unaware of our own blind spots. Therefore, we need indicators outside of ourselves to reveal to us that which is in our own heart. A good indicator is how your spouse reacts to the things you love.

For example, if a husband loves sports too much, his wife quite naturally will begin despising those sports. Similarly, the man who has an old buddy (whom his wife hates) probably is valuing that relationship too highly. What the wife hates really is not the buddy, but the fact that the buddy holds a place in her husband's heart that should belong to her. She feels violated and she, in fact, is being cheated. Whenever one person starts elevating in his or her heart something or someone in a wrong way, the married partner very commonly will begin to reject and despise that very thing or person.

We also saw this truth in the last chapter, as we explained how a Christian may exalt ministry to the place of an idol, and, therefore, the spouse wants nothing to do with it. If you understand this principle, you can be more in tune with yourself. Whenever you see your spouse "hating" something you do, check to see if you have excessive affection for that very thing.

We can learn more about *ourselves* by watching our mate than we can learn about *them*. The mirror image truth also can be seen in marriages where one person is a dreamer and the other is very practical. The more that one person focuses on all the hopeful possibilities, the more the other will focus on the practical aspects. This is not meant to make things difficult, creating all kinds of disagreements. On the contrary, if they learn to trust each other, this makes the best possible team.

What we need to watch for is polarization. If you have a disagreement with your mate, and he or she seems to be going to an extreme, you can bet that your own perception is equally as extreme in the opposite direction. When one person polarizes on one side of an issue, the other person will be polarizing on the other side.

IF YOUR SPOUSE
IS POLARIZING,
SO ARE YOU

Usually, neither realizes what he or she is doing. They see it from their own personal perspectives, but neither really is seeing the situation accurately. Therefore, when you see your spouse exaggerating some point, you can be pretty sure that you, in fact, are exaggerating in the opposite direction.

In counseling couples, I discovered a long time ago that if married people tell two different stories, pointing to two different extremes, you usually can average the two and find the truth. For example, if she says they have sexual relations every night, and he says they only have sex once every ten days, the truth will be somewhere around the five-day mark. Sometimes men like to think of themselves as more levelheaded in such areas, but I find both men and women equally subject to the polarization principle.

What I am saying is that *you can be deceived.* Your own perspective can be wrong. And the best indicator as to whether you are exaggerating things in your own mind is whether or not your spouse is exaggerating them in the opposite direction. The wise person learns about himself by watching his mate.

You can save yourself a lot of pain by being sensitive to this principle when making decisions. If your tightwad spouse says $50 is too much and you are willing to pay $100, probably $75 will be just about right. God puts tightwads and spenders together so they will be of help to each other—not hurt one another. The only difference between those who fight and those who take advantage of their difference is trust. Believing that your mate is God's perfect complement for you is the key to a blessed marriage.

If two people agree on everything, one of them is unnecessary. That's right. Having two different perspectives on things is what makes you able to work better as a team than individually. The fact is, you are attracted in the first place to someone who has the gifts and abilities in which you are weak. This, added to the molding power which is at work in you and your spouse, makes you perfect for each other. Let me say that again: you two are perfect for each other.

Not only can you make decisions more wisely, but you also can draw upon the other's strengths. To show you the reality of this, I would like to share from my own life a difference that my wife and I had which, rather than driving us apart, made us each better individuals.

When Linda and I met, she was very outgoing. I, on the other hand, was very reserved and quiet. In group situations, Linda seemed to me to be the loudest one present. In stores, while standing at the checkout counter, she typically got into a conversation with whomever else was waiting in line. She loved to talk and reveal things about her own life. Unfortunately, that was beginning to include my life, and I preferred having no one know anything except what I chose to have revealed. Please do not take me wrong concerning my sweetheart. She was loved by everyone and a joy to be with. I, however, was the one who had to learn how to deal with her outgoing personality.

During our courtship I tried all the wrong ways to change Linda. I frequently discussed with her the value of quieting down. I tried to sound my sternest when telling her that my life was none of anyone else's business. I continued along those lines, but nothing seemed to produce the results I desired. Finally, I simply avoided being in group situations with her.

It was not until I changed myself that she changed. I started realizing that Linda had a lot more fun in life than I did. Basically, I was an insecure, stick-in-the-mud. I saw that the very thing that attracted me to her in the

first place was, in part, this gift which I had been despising. I started to admit to myself that her outgoing
nature was not all bad, and I was the one in greater need
of change. Even though it hurt when she exposed some
new area of my life, I started saying to myself, "Harold,
this is good for you! You need to open yourself up!" It
was not easy, but I determined to make myself more
outgoing. I was not as good at it as Linda was, and at
times I felt as though I was pretending or forcing myself
in group situations. It was hard. Change always is. But
I did succeed in changing myself.

Today, my wife is friendly but not excessively outgoing. Only about one in three times does she start a
conversation while standing at the checkout counter.
I do it once in a while myself, now. It is kind of fun. My
real character changes are seen in larger groups. If you
knew me personally, you would know that I am known
as a bold person. It was not all my efforts that brought
forth those changes. My wife simultaneously worked at
subduing the energy in her. I received some of that
energy. It came into me. She is one of the reasons I am
able to carry on a decent conversation today. Part of
her nature was imparted into me. Today, we are both
more the way God wants us to be.

As we said, people initially are attracted to a mate
who has the very traits they lack. If we fight those
qualities in our spouse, they only will be amplified and
cause greater difficulties. If, however, we allow ourselves
to become one without reservations, and draw within
ourselves those characteristics, they, indeed, will be
incorporated and added into our lives. At the same time,
excesses will be removed from our mate. This is how
a person becomes complete in marriage.

Finally, I want to explain that marriage is the best
place to learn how to communicate. This is the most

important ability you will learn in life. If you can share your heart in the security of your home, you will advance far in your enjoyment of life. If you never know how to share your joys and blessings with another person, you never will enjoy them yourself to the fullest.

If you can learn how to converse, you will advance far in marital blessing and, ultimately, in all of life. Communication takes disciplining yourself. It is a process. It is the most important ability you can master this side of the grave.

Success in life is not based on *what you know* as much as it is determined by *how you think.* For example, we all have heard of the two different views people have when they see a half-filled glass of water. Some people optimistically will say that the glass is half full, while others will say that the glass is half empty. Both groups of people have the same information, but their perspectives are different. It is not what people *know* that primarily determines the quality of their lives, but rather their *perspective* and *how they think* about the reality around them.

This is evident in marriage perhaps more than any other place. How a couple thinks determines everything. For example, we tried earlier in this book to change people's concept of love. People who think that love is some magical, out-of-control force live as victims, not knowing how to improve their marriage or ever experiencing the emotions of love again. On the other hand, people who understand that love can be kindled by exposing their hearts one to another realize that a successful marriage is simply a matter of their own will.

How couples think about each other also determines their enjoyment of marriage. Every couple has differences. If they perceive of those differences as curses to be resisted and despised, then they will have problems throughout their lives. If, on the other hand, they look at those differences as opportunities, then great blessing can come forth and actually make life a lot better. Marriage is your best opportunity to change yourself for the better. You choose whether or not to take that opportunity or let it pass by. This is how to think.

Attitudes Toward Headship

A final biblical concept which we must consider is
headship. It is my hope that in the remaining pages you
will see this subject in a totally new light that will create
liberty for you.

In the New Testament, the Apostle Paul laid out the
principles of headship. He wrote:

> . . . Christ is the head of every man, and the
> man is the head of a woman, and God is the
> head of Christ.
>
> I Cor. 11:3

Some people have misinterpreted such Bible verses and
taken them to unbiblical extremes, leading to domina-
tion and oppression. Others have denied the related
truths altogether. Since God inspired teachings about
headship in several Old Testament and New Testament
passages, we would be foolish to reject them. It is proper
application that will bring blessings to the marital relationship.

Do not think of the Bible writers as male chauvinists.

Closer examination reveals just the opposite. Chauvinism sees women as inferior to men. The Bible does not teach that.

The Bible portrays the godly woman as one who is fully capable, both in the home and in the business world. Proverbs 31 describes the "excellent wife" to us. This woman, put forth in the Bible as a standard, was investing in real estate (31:16), hiring workers, running a farm, and increasing in wealth by actively producing trade items (31:16,24). The godly woman of Proverbs, we are told, even was known "in the gates" for her works, which meant that she was so productive that the leaders of the city respected her (31:31). She is shown as managing her home well (31:15-28), not afraid of the outside world or the future (31:21, 25), full of wisdom (31:26), and girding herself with strength (31:17). This is a woman, we are told, who excels above all others (31:29). She is not depicted as an unusual woman, but as a role model for all women to emulate.

The Bible image of the woman's role is not sitting at home in a helpless, less-than-fulfilled lifestyle. Nor does it portray women as less intelligent than men. Male chauvinism, on the other hand, makes such false judgments. Make no mistake about this. The Bible is not chauvinistic. It does *not* consider women as "second-class citizens."

Nor is a man the head of a woman because women possess less of God's blessings or gifts. Throughout history, we have seen women being used by God to accomplish some of the most significant feats and achievements. In Galatians 3, we read what Paul has to say concerning our inheritance as Christians and the workings of the Holy Spirit. In these respects, Paul wrote that ". . . there is neither male nor female; for you are all one in Christ Jesus" (Gal. 3:28). As far as anointings are concerned, God gives them to both men and women. There is a divine order of headship, but it does not exist because women are any less gifted by the Holy Spirit.

Then, how should we understand the order of headship? After stating the divine order in I Cor. 11:3, Paul went on to give us four reasons why this order exists. He explained that the man is the head of the woman . . .

1. . . . since he is the image and glory of God; but the woman is the glory of man.
2. For man does not originate from woman, but woman from man;
3. for indeed man was not created for woman's sake, but woman for the man's sake.
4. . . . because of the angels.

I Cor. 11:7-10

Notice that all four of these reasons point back to how God created men and women. We are told that man is the head of woman because he was "created" in the image and glory of God, while the woman was created in the glory of man; second, that the woman "originated" from man; and third, that the woman was "created" for man's sake. All these reasons point back to how God established things in the beginning. They point to His intentions and purposes. The fourth reason, "because of the angels," also is related to Creative design, but we will address it in the next chapter. The reason divine order exists is because God created it that way in the beginning.

Many Christians today are confused concerning why this order is given to us in the Bible. They never have studied the Bible carefully to see why or when it came into being. Not understanding that God established it at Creation, they typically have misconceptions and sometimes conclude that it was taught in the Bible for one of the following erroneous reasons.

Some Christians incorrectly think that men were placed over women in the Bible because the society in which the Bible writers lived was male dominated. It is true that men played the dominant role in Bible times, but that is not the reason that Paul told us that men are to be the head. He did not say, "Men are the head because society dictates it." On the contrary, he told us it was because in the beginning God established it that way. All the reasons given by Paul point to God's creative purposes and desires, which apply to all societies of all times. Paul was not adjusting to the society around him. Likewise, as Bible-believing Christians today, we should be convinced that society around us must adjust to biblical standards, not the other way around.

Another misconception sometimes held by Christians today is that the headship role of men was the result of Eve's sin. They wrongly conclude that the curse which was placed upon mankind because of the fall (Gen. 3:16-19) included the rulership of men over women. Because they perceive of the curse as evil, they conclude, therefore, that the headship role of men should be overcome and conquered, rather than something to which you yield in today's world. Of course, there were devastating effects of the fall in relation to the roles of men and women, which we will discuss later, but at this point we must recognize that divine order is not the result of Eve's sin . . . nor Adam's. The Bible teaches that this order was established by God at Creation, before Adam and Eve sinned.

Divine order simply *exists*. It exists because that is the way God ordered things in the beginning. It is by

His design.

ORDER EXISTS:

GOD
|
CHRIST
|
MAN
|
WOMAN

God did not do away with this order in the New Testament, nor at any other time. That is made obvious by the Apostle Paul's explanation of the order being given to us in the New Testament; hence, we cannot deny that it applies directly to us.

Some Christians have misunderstood Paul's exhortation in Gal. 3:28 (which tells us that there is no male nor female) as relating to the divine order. This verse is in the context of both men and women being heirs of God's promises and the Holy Spirit. Of course, women, as well as men, can accomplish great works by the power of the Holy Spirit. There is no male nor female in respect to our experience of the Holy Spirit or obtaining His blessings. However, does not change the divine order. The fact that Jesus was full of the Spirit in no way disrupted His place in the divine order under the Father. Similarly, both men and women in the Lord are priests unto God, and they can share equally in the Holy Spirit, but this in no way changes the order established by God at Creation. The work of the Spirit in our lives is not to undo God's will, but to help us fulfill it.

Then, how do we apply headship and see it realized today?

Confusion in this area simply stems from misunderstanding what headship is. Paul gave us the model in the book of Ephesians where he writes concerning *how* a man is to be the head of his wife.

> For the husband is the head of the wife, as
> Christ also is the head of the church. . . .
> Eph. 5:23

The pattern from which a man can learn how to be the head is in the relationship Jesus has with the Church. Jesus is portrayed as the Husband to a Bride. Paul said that *in this same way,* the husband is the head of the wife.

Examine, therefore, the relationship Jesus has to His Bride. He is not dominating, nor legalistically forcing Her into submission. On the contrary, His influence primarily is through the sanctifying work of Him becoming one with Her. Even more important is that our Lord's ultimate goal for His Bride is to elevate Her that

JESUS   **CHURCH**

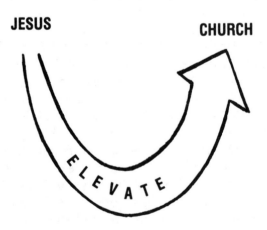

She might rule and reign with Him. Jesus has accomplished the work for which He came to the world, but He intends to work out His ongoing purposes through His Church. He desires to impart His authority to Her. She is called a co-heir with Him in all things. Jesus is the Head, but His overall plan is to bring the Church alongside of Himself in all that He does.

Since this is the example the Bible gives us of what headship is, the man of today is wise to take note. His position is not one of controlling "his woman," but of *becoming one* in thoughts, desires, and goals with his wife. The man of God elevates his wife to his side. He sees her as capable and intelligent. He values her judgment and trusts her (Prov. 31:11). The blessed marriage is one wherein the husband looks to his wife for help in handling all the affairs of their lives.

Step back and look at the overall picture the Bible gives us. In the beginning God created Adam and Eve. He gave them authority over the earth and told them to rule and reign together (Gen. 1:28). Adam and Eve failed and submitted their lives to Satan. In I Corinthians 15, Jesus Christ is referred to as the "Last Adam." A comparison is made there between the first Adam, who failed, and Jesus Christ, Who accomplished the will of the Father. The first Adam was a natural human being, but the Last Adam was the Son of God. The Last is raising a Bride for Himself. Jesus Christ will rule and reign with His Bride, according to the will of the Father.

The spirit of the first Adam is different than the Spirit of the Last. The first sinned, and his relationship with his wife became one characteristic of the words within the curse, "He shall rule over you" (Gen. 3:16). Sin brought in the attitude of men dominating and oppressing women. That is evil. In contrast, the Spirit of the Last Adam desires to elevate His Bride and lift Her up to walk alongside of Him. Male chauvinism is a result of Adam's sin. A husband/wife relationship wherein the man exalts his wife to his side is the pattern of Jesus Christ.

**THE SPIRIT OF
JESUS IN
MARRIAGE**

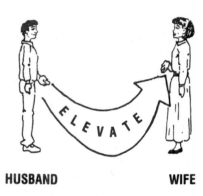

HUSBAND   **WIFE**

The *godly* attitude a man should have toward his wife is to treat her "as a fellow heir of the grace of life" (I Pet. 3:7). This is the Spirit of Jesus toward His Bride. This is what husbands are to emulate.

We also must identify the proper attitude of a wife toward her husband. When we look again at the relationship between our Lord and the Church, we see that the Church, indeed, will be exalted to our Lord's right hand and She will share in His authority. However, She is not to demand that position from Him. She receives it. As the Body of Christ emulates the character and heart of the Lord, She automatically rises in authority and majesty.

It is in a corresponding fashion that a woman is to submit to her husband. She must endeavor to bring her labors in line with his will. She is to please him. She will be blessed if she represents his nature and reflects what he believes and that for which he stands. Paul explained it by saying that a wife is to portray her husband's glory (I Cor. 11:7). A wife will receive her husband's authority when she receives his heart. This is the focus for the godly woman.

The Apostle Peter taught the same principles. He exhorted the women to be submissive to their own husbands, looking to Sarah as a model of how to conduct themselves.

> Thus Sarah obeyed Abraham, calling him lord, and you have become her children if you do what is right without being frightened by any fear.
>
> I Pet. 3:6

Peter commended the women of God and described the "gentle and quiet spirit, which is precious in the sight of God" (I Pet. 3:4). This is the pattern for the godly woman.

We are speaking here of attitudes and motivatons. The attitude of a woman to exalt herself is not of God. Nor is the downgrading of women by men a godly practice. Both feminism and male chauvinism are evil. They are from the spirit of the natural world. No matter what you have been taught or what you have seen in society around you, make no mistake about what the Bible teaches. The Spirit of God is that which causes a man to exalt his wife and a wife to yield to her husband's authority.

In writing these things, I wish we could address husbands and wives individually. It is not the husband's job to make his wife submit. Nor is it the wife's job to make her husband exalt her. If the wife simply keeps her focus on what she is supposed to do, it releases the hand of God to begin forming her husband. So, also, if the husband is attempting to become one with his wife and elevate her, then the Spirit of God is able to work more freely in her, to make her a wife who will want to please him. A man has no right waiting for his wife to be submissive before he exalts her. No. His job is to take the initiative, as Jesus did toward the Church, and become one with his wife. If husbands would do what they are supposed to do and wives what they are called to do, God would take care of their mates. The focus is on *you*.

The issue here is the right heart attitude. You may have questions arising in your mind about specific practical applications, but please direct your attention toward your own heart. If you will forget all the superficial questions, you will be able simply to humble your heart, which is precisely what is needed. When the hearts are right, the actions will be right.

God has designed the man to be the head and the woman to be at his side. A man never will be happy or blessed while he is dominating his wife (I Pet. 3:7). A woman never can be fulfilled unless she is at her husband's side. She is created to be busy and to exercise authority over the affairs of life. However, it is not enough for a woman to have a career and be busy. Unless she is submitted in heart to her husband, she will be empty in what she does. A woman finds fulfillment through her labors, but they must be brought in line with the one to whom she has joined herself. A husband must elevate his wife to his side as an equal. He must provide leadership and direction. We will describe this more fully in the next chapter, but know at this point that this is the biblical picture of headship.

Chapter 14

The Way Things Work

In the last chapter we explained the headship relation which God has established between a man and a woman. We saw that this was instituted in the beginning and it exists by Creative design. Please make no mistake about what the Bible teaches. There is an authority structure. Now, let's understand it more clearly and see how it may be realized in our daily lives.

Sometimes Christians confuse where this "headship" applies. For example, my wife Linda always has kept our children's need in high priority, but she also has held various types of employment over the past few years. If I showed up where she worked, it would be wrong for me to expect her undivided attention. I am not head of her place of employment. Her boss is. When I am there, I have to submit to that authority structure.

This truth also can be brought into our home. Notice that the Bible no where says, "The man is the head of the home." That is a Christian cliche that is not in the Bible, but some Christians still use it. What the Bible says is that the man is the head of the wife (Eph. 5:23; I Cor. 11:3). There is a big difference.

In my home, there are many ways in which I am submitted to my wife. For example, in our home it is
primarily my wife who sets the schedule for meals,
cleaning, when the children get up, and most of the
other domestic affairs. Basically, she runs our home.
When I am trying to help her with the house cleaning
or laundry or some other aspect of home life, I submit
to her. I fit into her schedule and planning, as far as
home management is concerned. Not all marriages are
run as ours, but please realize that the Bible *does not*
say, "The man is the head of the home."

What does the Bible tell us? "The man is the head
of the woman"(I Cor. 11:3; Eph. 5:23). The headship
role exists in the *relationship,* not in any particular or
singular setting of life. It is in the overall plan of life
that a woman's work and home management should
be brought into line with the direction and course which
her husband is going. It is in this sense that the man
is the head.

When the Bible tells us that a man is the head, it is
describing a relationship which simply exists.

> The husband is the head.
>
> Eph. 5:23

This is stated as matter-of-factly as one might say, "The
sky is blue." The Bible is not instructing us to try to
force this kind of relationship into being. No. It already
exists. The Bible simply is reporting to us the facts.

The headship role of a man is a state of being which
cannot be altered, nor are we to strive to establish it.
The truth is that it already has been established. Just
as God said, "Let there be light," so also He decreed
and established a relationship between a man and
woman, sustained by His power. No human being is big
enough to change this. There is a law—unbreakable,

inescapable—which established an order between man and woman.

GOD

"THE MAN IS THE HEAD"

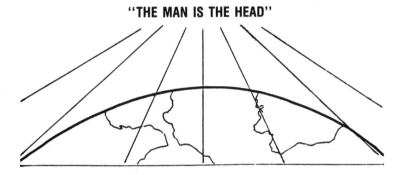

Not perceiving the reality of this power, many men "try to become the head," rather than recognizing that they already are the head. When a man tries to force himself into this position, rather than acknowledge it, he makes a mess of things. This will become clear as we continue.

Women, misunderstanding the preexisting state of headship, equally can make a mess of their marriage. Please look at Eph. 5:22,23 from a new perspective.

> Wives, be subject to your own husbands, as to the Lord. For the husband is the head of the wife, as Christ also is the head of the church....

Do we question Christ's headship of the Church? No. We know that whenever Christians try to do something apart from the leading and direction of Jesus, they do not produce lasting fruit. In the same way, the husband, we are told, is the head of the woman.

Let me give you an example of how this works. Many wives have tried to do something such as train their children along certain lines, even though their husbands were not in agreement. All too often I have seen that if a wife tries to steer her children in a specific direction contrary to her husband's desires, sooner or later her labors prove vain.

Consider for a moment the family in which the mother spends years raising her children according to a godly pattern: taking them to church, talking to them about the Lord regularly, etc. Then picture the non-Christian husband sitting in his easy chair, one day calling his teenage son over and saying, "Your mother is just a Jesus freak and you don't need to listen to her anymore." With one such statement, a man can undo what his wife has spent years trying to accomplish.

Even though the husband may not be involved actively with the work of his wife, his agreement in heart binds or looses the power of God, which makes his wife effective over the long term. We are not saying this to discourage wives, but to open people's eyes to see how they can work *with* God's power, rather than *against* it.

When Paul exhorted wives to submit to their husbands, he was not giving a legalistic command. Rather, it was an explanation. He said to submit because "the husband is the head." We can put it in perspective by illustrating it with a woman standing on the side of a hill, about to roll a huge rock up or down hill; wise counsel would tell her to roll the rock downhill because it is easier. It is in this manner that Paul wrote, "Submit, because men are the head." A smart wife will bring her actions in line with her husband's desires, because then God's authority will work with her, rather than against her. These things are explained to make life easier, better, more blessed.

This gives us an understanding of Paul's words, ". . . because of the angels" (I Cor. 11:10), which he gave as one of the reasons for headship. The Bible explains that angels minister to us and serve us (Heb. 1:14). Of course, they will not violate God's authority structure. Psalms 103:20 tells us that angels perform God's word. Romans 13:1 tells us that all the authorities which exist are established by God. Angels, therefore, will not act against God's design. They do, however, help us according to the will of God when our lives are in line with His will. Paul was explaining to us that angelic ministry and the very blessings of God upon our marriages are dependent upon our functioning according to divine order.

I have observed this principle functioning where women have tried to accomplish great things in the church. As a minister, I have known several women who have very bold, out-front ministries. I am not saying anything negative about women being on the forefront, because I believe God, by His Spirit, empowers and distributes His gifts to women, as well as to men. I have been instrumental personally in helping several women into Christian ministries. I believe in women doing great works for God in the earth.

However, I have observed that if a gifted woman does not have her husband's support, what she tries to achieve tends not to stand the test of time. By her determination and strength of character, she can force certain ministries to progress, but as soon as she "lets down," powers immediately start decaying her accomplishments. It is supernatural. In contrast, it does not happen in the ministries of men to anywhere near the same extent. A woman needs a man's covering, and without it she is subject to tremendous pressure and stresses, which work both on her and her ministry.

A woman can be successful if her husband has locked in his heart a support and agreement for his wife's labors. That husband may not even like to speak in front of crowds or be on the forefront in any way. However, his believing in his wife releases her to be effective. He has a very real authority which is evident. Even the non-Christian husband seems to have a certain authority to release blessing upon his wife's labors, simply by the attitude of his heart to bless her. Because the man is the head, he has the authority to bind or loose.

Attention is not called to this so that women in ministry will rebuke their nonsupportive husbands. That is contrary to what we are teaching. It is not just support she needs. Headship already exists. She needs to bring her life into alignment with divine order.

Authority and headship are real. When the Centurion came to Jesus, he said that he was a man under authority, and because he also had authority over others, he understood authority (Matt. 8:5-13). With this understanding, the Centurion said to Jesus that all He would have to do is speak a word and God's authority would be released. People today similarly must understand God-ordained authority. It exists between a man and a woman. It is the way things work.

In teaching here about authority, we need to see that authority flows not only through the family, but in other areas of life, as well. For example, earlier I mentioned my wife's previous employment. Her authority on the job is delegated to her from her boss. In the Church, there exists another line of authority established by God, and church leaders should, therefore, be especially sensitive to extend the Church's authority to cover and support women who have no husband to bless their labors. We do not want you to think that all authority comes through the family. There are many forms of authority, and all people are intersubmitted in numerous ways. We simply are showing one very real line which does exist between husbands and wives.

We cannot end this discussion without a final exhortation to men concerning the God-given role which is theirs. Speaking to men, let me say that no matter what you have heard, no matter what the world has tried to portray as today's man, do not be confused about who you are. The macho image depicted by many modern movies, wherein the male hero acts alone and independently—yet always gets his lady—is a lie. So also is the other extreme of a man who is weak and unable to make decisions. Women never have and never will admire wimps. Headship is leadership. Make no mistake about this. God has given you, oh man, the position of authority. Therefore, you must step into your God-ordained place.

That headship position is a place of responsibility. The word "authority" translated into everyday lingo means "responsibility." The two are inseparable.

Several elements are key in this. It involves keeping a perspective of your marriage and family whereby you can keep the bigger picture in focus and see where your lives are going. Leadership demands taking time to think about and plan where you are going and what must be done to accomplish your goals. It is impossible to be a godly head, or any kind of head, for that matter, unless you accept the responsibility and actually take on an objective, long-range view of your lives. Nothing frustrates a woman more than trying to follow a man who has neglected to spend time thinking about where he is going himself. Of course, there may be temporary periods of transition during which direction is unclear, but overall, the plans must be communicated and kept in mind by the one called to be the head. This is what it means to be a head. This is the definition. The man who does not accept this responsibility either never has been taught these truths, or he is just lazy and needs to be harshly rebuked.

Headship also involves accepting responsibility for the overall success or failure of the marriage and family. A man may delegate to his wife various aspects of management, but ultimately, he holds the final responsibility before God.

The man was designed by God for this task. A woman is not designed to carry the load of responsibility. We are told that women are created "for man" (I Cor. 11:9) and as a helpmeet (Gen. 2:18). They are weaker vessels (I Pet. 3:7), not in the sense of being inferior or less intelligent or less capable in life. But they are designed by the Master Architect to stay under a man's care and covering. An automobile is designed to transport people. A house is designed as a place in which people will live. And a man is designed to carry the load of responsibility, while a woman is not.

This means that if things are too stressful for a wife, a godly husband will step in and lift the load. If rearing the children is too difficult in some area, he must be there to relieve her. The financial successes and failures of the family are dependent ultimately upon the man. A woman can and should help out in providing materially, but she should not carry the weight of thinking their subsistance is dependent upon her paycheck. On a regular basis, a wife must be able to give up her load and put it back into her husband's hands. She needs to be taken out on a date now and then, so she can forget all of her responsibilities and be reminded that her husband is there. And, of course, he needs to be there.

It is before God that a man is responsible. The Bible

teaches us that even though Eve ate of the forbidden tree first, it was Adam who was held responsible for allowing sin to enter the world (Rom. 5:12-19). Every husband and father will be held accountable by God for the family over which they have been put in charge. Simply realizing this fact should create a seriousness in every man. The one who has a careless attitude in these matters is being unfaithful in his God-given responsibility

(Some wives may read these exhortations I am directing toward men and become stirred in anger toward their husbands who are not measuring up. I am being very bold here concerning the man's role, because of so much confusion in today's modern world. However, none of these points are given so a wife has ammunition against her man. If a woman wants to change her irresponsible husband, I would direct her back to chapters ten and eleven, where we discussed change in marriage.)

When a man accepts responsibility, the ability to lead is activated. A man is a leader by Creative design. Within his nature is the ability to be the head. Just as a mother has an instinctive knowledge concerning how to care for her children, so also a man has a built-in guidance system as to how he should lead his family. When he steps into the responsibility given to him, those gifts within are released and activated spontaneously.

I have observed again and again profound wisdom coming forth from husbands who have accepted responsibility for their families. Even in cases where the father is a non-Christian and the rest of the family is saved, God uses the man to lead if he has stepped into his ordained role. Authority, wisdom, direction, and the ability to make decisions are given supernaturally to the man who rises and accepts responsibility.

Therefore, a man must learn to trust the gifts and calling within himself. A husband who has accepted responsibility will have the hand of God urging him to do what must be done during the course of life. It is the authority of God which reveals to a man everything he needs to know to direct his family. In other words, it is God who is at work within the man, urging him to make decisions and give direction. God gives the man answers when faced with problems. Thoughts come spontaneously. If a man realizes that it is, indeed, God's authority at work on his behalf, then he will have confidence to step out and be the head he was created to be. If, however, he does not understand that it is his God-given gift to lead, then he will doubt himself and be indecisive. (So also, if a wife does not understand the God-ordained nature of her husband, she will doubt his leadership.) Therefore, men (and women) must be taught clearly that the headship gifts within the man are God-given and can be trusted. Of course, he can make mistakes, but understanding this truth builds confidence in a father and it brings security to the family.

To the husbands, let me speak more directly. That which urges you to do this or that is the authority with which you were created. We, of course, are not justifying your every whim or desire, but rather we recognize that you as a man are creatively designed to lead. It is natural for you. Other tendencies are unnatural. Therefore, you must have confidence in the decisions you make. God has chosen you, appointed you, and designed you to be the head.

Finally, listen to your wife, husband. The insecure man tends to think that if he listens to his wife he will be controlled by her. That is ridiculous. The more you expose your heart, listen to, and become one with your wife, the more the spiritual relationship ordained by God becomes manifest. It is the very molding power of God which causes your wife to become a suitable helper for you. The wife who is given her rightful place alongside her husband, automatically and supernaturally begins to elevate and build up her man. Knowing this, men need not be afraid. There is nothing that can change your preexisting, God-established position. You are the head. God said it. . . therefore, it exists.

When you listen to your wife, you are not listening to a foreigner. The Bible says, "He who loves his own wife loves himself" (Eph. 5:28b). Your wife is a part of you. She is, in fact, you. You are her. She is God's complement to you. The reason she has something to say is because God's power is at work in her, opening her eyes to see what you cannot see. When you listen to your wife, you are listening to the part of you of which you presently may not be conscious.

Society today sometimes portrays and pushes relationships contrary to the biblical pattern. Do not be deceived. Those marriages are cursed. It is true today, as it has been in all ages, that the man is the head. The godly marriage is one wherein a man acts confidently as head, listens to his wife, and supports her in the endeavors of life as she brings her labors under his headship. This marriage will be blessed.

Chapter 15

Exactly What to Do!

When I look at marriages today, my heart breaks.
There is such confusion and turmoil that I am moved
to intercession and prayer. As I travel and speak in
churches in many regions, I see people in situations that
seem hopeless, apart from God's intervention. Even
Christian marriages are under severe attack. The devil
is active and the spirit of the world is taking its toll.

I would like to express my sympathy to every person
in marital conflict, but I believe that even more than
expressions of concern, Christians today need to be told
simply and clearly to grow up, stop doing what the world
is doing, and start loving each other. If you can receive
this properly, I would like to say that most married
people could solve 99% of their difficulties, if they
simply would do what the Bible tells them to do.

Jesus said it best (Matt. 7:24-27). He described the
foolish man who hears the words of God but does not
apply them. He compared that man with a person who
built his house upon sand, and when the rains and winds

came, the house was destroyed. In contrast, another man who was wise built his house upon solid rock, and nothing could shake that house. This second man, our Lord explained, is like the one who hears and obeys, and, as a result, is blessed.

In this book, we have explained many principles from the Bible concerning marriage. I am fearful that some will read these pages, say, "That's nice," and then put them aside, as the foolish man our Lord described. Perhaps it is because I do not want my own words tossed aside. On the other hand, it may be because my heart truly is breaking for marriages that I cannot bear to see these words wasted. If what Jesus said was true, then application, rather than reading, brings blessings.

We have dealt with three foundational principles to a good marriage. First, we explained how God's force which binds two people together can be released, causing them to fall in love with a rekindling of the romance and emotions they once had for each other. Second, we taught on how a marriage can be released from the curse of the law and brought into the blessings of grace. And finally, we discussed divine order, which brings harmony and fulfilled purpose in marriage.

I want to be sure you heard those words. I do not want you to close this book without a realization concerning how a good marriage works. I especially want to make sure that you understand that it is *you* who decides whether or not the fire will be burning in your marriage. There *is* something you actually can do about it.

Of course, application is harder than reading. For example, when I suggested that every couple get away from their daily concerns and go on a date, I suppose resisting thoughts arose in many readers' minds. Couples who read this book together probably have passing romantic thoughts, but one or the other partner may have hurried through those portions, lest they be confronted by their negligence. You see, application will mean that you have to rearrange the priorities of your life. That's the problem: married couples frequently come asking for help in their relationship, but when you tell them that the answer is to make their relationship a priority, they say, "Thank you, but no thanks." What they really wanted was an answer that did not require them to do anything.

I am amazed at how many couples put out the minimum energy necessary to just barely keep their marriage afloat. Is anyone out there listening? Your marriage will cost you. It takes an output of energy. If you want it to be better, you will have to do *something* differently than you are right now. *You will have to change.*

So why not change? Yes, just change. Isn't that a great idea?

Husbands, why don't you just start loving your wives? Shock her. Take off work early and treat her differently—better—for an evening. Write her a love note and leave it under her pillow. Take her in your arms and make her feel cared for.

To make life simple, men, you must understand what a woman desires and needs. The Apostle Paul exhorted husbands to nourish and cherish their wives (Eph. 5:29). Your wife needs to be cared for. She needs financial and emotional security.

A woman's desire for security is God-given. Her desire for a home, bills paid, food in the kitchen, and constant assurance of your love is not because of any lack of faith or because of any selfishness on her part. This is how God made her. Birds need air in which to fly. Plants need sunlight, water, and good soil. And wives need an atmosphere of security in which to live.

If a man will provide financial and emotional security for his wife, he will create an environment in which she will flourish and become what he desires. This is a promise of God:

> *When you shall eat of the fruit of your hands,*
> *You will be happy and it will be well with you.*
> *Your wife shall be like a fruitful vine*
> *Within your house,*
> *Your children like olive plants*
> *Around your table.*
>
> Psalms 128:2,3

A promise is made here of a wife becoming as a "fruitful vine" and the blessings extend to the children and entire home life. However, this promise (as are many others) is conditional. It is not for the man who refuses to work or is lazy. It is not for those who live off of the government or others. God promised to bless the man who works and provides for his household.

Flowers bloom in a warm greenhouse, colorful fish thrive along the coral beaches of Australia, and families become healthy in an environment of financial and emotional security.

It is vital that men learn this basic lesson of life. From young ages, boys should be taught to be security-providers, promise-keepers, and lovers. Training, hard work, and proving faithful on a job are essentials for well-being. Of course, there are special needs and temporary seasons in which a father may be unable to bless his family financially. But overall through the course of life, a man must accept this responsibility for his wife and children. Too much confusion has gone on in our society concerning these issues. It is time we praise the father and husband who faithfully provides for his children year after year and stays true to his wife.

Finally, men, let me talk to you in words that you can understand. Most likely you take care of your car by putting in gas and oil regularly. Also, you willingly take your vehicle in for a tune-up now and then, and perhaps an occasional wash and shine. Well, your wife needs gas and oil. What keeps her running are financial provisions and your love. She also needs a regular tune-up, which only happens at a restaurant, over dinner, away from the children, with your undivided attention. You put the shine on her face when the words come out of your mouth, "Honey, you are beautiful." Take better care of your wife than you do your car. Any questions?

In exhorting the wives, I would like to borrow the words which Linda, my wife, often gives to women complaining to her about their unresponsive husbands, non-Christian husbands, and husbands who will not communicate. She says, "You know exactly what to do!" I want you to receive this with the same impact that she would say it to you. So please imagine her sitting right there with you in your room and telling it to you face to face with all the conviction and determination in her heart. She knows what she is talking about—believe me.

A woman is born with a certain "know-how" concerning how to influence men. That's a fact which you immediately learn when you have a daughter. Girls come out at birth knowing how to influence their dad. As the Bible says, the woman was created for the sake of the man (I Cor. 11:9), and, therefore, when she grows up and gets married, she has what it takes to fulfill, complement, and satisfy her husband. That is how God created women.

If you have blocked out of your mind how you can win your husband's heart, then let me jog your memory. Picture the average businessman in your town who is surrounded by young secretaries. When one of those secretaries sets her sights on that boss, what does she do? Think about it. I mean seriously—think about it. How would she make herself look? If that secretary were trying to get *your* husband, what would she do? That's exactly what you need to do to solve your problem.

Think for a moment about Delilah in the Bible (Judges 16). She was able to extract from Samson his deepest, innermost secrets, upon which his own life depended. Of course, Delilah was wrong in what she did. What I want you to recognize, though, is the influence a woman can have in a man's life if she really wants to. Jesus pointed out that the children of this world are more shrewd in dealing with others than the children of light (Luke 16:8). Sometimes Christian women—in their desire to be godly—forget how to be a woman. You were creatively designed by God knowing how to reach your husband's heart. Those abilities were not given to you to use on any other man, and they were not given to you so you will bury them. Men have a weak spot—it gives them pleasure to have you fit into that spot. They were designed by God to need you there.

If you want your husband's heart, then go get it. Stop making excuses. It is that simple. Back to the counsel of my wife: "Every woman knows what to do, but most of them are just unwilling to do it." They are simply too lazy to win their own husband. She said it, not me. But she's right!

To the wives I would like to say, "It is time to get it together and redirect your life." Stop acting like a victim or thinking of yourself as powerless. Remember when you first won his heart? Remember that look you put on your face? Go ahead and put it on again. It has not been that long. Direct your energy toward your man tonight. Become creative. No more "same ole, same ole." Put a smile on his face. You know you can win his heart again if you want to. Put on some makeup and look good for him. He will start talking to you again if you really want him to talk.

This is precisely what Jesus was talking about. Do not be a hearer of these things, but a doer. Hearers' houses crumble sooner or later. Doers receive blessings and build houses that stand through trials. Do you want to know why some marriages are happy today, while others around are falling apart? Application! Marriages *never* crumble because of financial difficulties, or in-law turmoil, or incompatibility problems, or any other natural thing. These are trials. The winds and the rains will come against *every* marriage. But houses do not stand because they were built on sand. The reason marriages fail is because the individuals involved were not building properly. In other words, they were not doing—applying—what they needed to do.

A secure house is not built overnight. It takes years for two people to be molded together into a stable, unshakable relationship. The molding process begins immediately, but the longer two people yield to its forces, the more they form into complementary parts that make an inseparable team.

Through experience, we know that there are critical points at which couples' lives are rapidly deepened one with another. Of course, the molding processes are intensified when they determine to go through stressful times together. But there are also natural breaking points that occur around the one-year, three-year, seven-year, fourteen-year, and twenty-one-year marks. For example, after a couple has been together for the first year, they seem to complete the first stage of their lives together, and their relationship takes on a new, deeper stability. Toward the end of their three-year milestone, they go through another transition that brings them to a new level of commitment, another plateau in their lives together. Time goes on, reaching deeper into their lives, extending the molding power again at every interval of seven years. It is just prior to these transitional points that couples often find themselves resisting each other and in conflict. Without being able to identify the reason, they feel themselves being pulled deeper and deeper into a supernatural oneness by the ongoing molding process. If they resist it, they resist God's power. If, however, they go on through each transition yielding more of themselves, they find themselves significantly more one with their spouse than previously.

What we are saying is that a good marriage takes years to develop. Marriage is for life. The key is to yield to God's molding power, rather than fight it.

Of course, there are trials in every marriage. Your problems would not be solved if you were married to Mr. Perfect or Mrs. Model-of-the-Year. Such people do not exist, anyway. Everyone has character flaws. If you already have a mate, then that person is the one who is being molded supernaturally according to your nature. Accept it. Marital blessings come not when you succeed in changing him or her, but when you get on the same wave length and embrace your mate as God's gift to you—imperfections and all.

Finally, let me say that a marriage is worth everything you put into it. It is the only thing you can keep all your life. Jobs change. Career plans go through transitions. Homes, cars, and other possessions pass on. Your children will leave home. Even your strength will not be with you always. But that one to whom you have committed your life will be there for years to come. Your spouse is by far your best investment. Nothing can give you more joy than a blessed marriage. Realize, though, that only what you actually apply builds the relationship on a solid foundation. Do not be deceived. You know exactly what to do!

Let me close by saying a prayer and releasing God's blessing upon your marriage and your home.

> *May the Lord God Almighty bless you and open your eyes to see how you can meet the needs of your spouse. May you have the desire to do so. I rebuke the enemy of men's souls from your life and marriage in the name of Jesus Christ. May the walls within your relationship crumble. And may the God of victory give you strength, romance, and intimacy. By His power let the two of you become one.*

Please receive this blessing as from the throne of God.

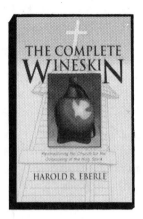